To Unite
the Scattered Children of God

To Unite the Scattered Children of God

Hope for the Spiritual Uniting of Humanity, from Isaiah to the Present Day

STEPHEN FINLAN

 CASCADE *Books* • Eugene, Oregon

TO UNITE THE SCATTERED CHILDREN OF GOD
Hope for the Spiritual Uniting of Humanity, from Isaiah to the Present Day

Cascade Books
An Imprint of Wipf and Stock Publishers
199 W. 8th Ave., Suite 3
Eugene, OR 97401

www.wipfandstock.com

PAPERBACK ISBN: 978-1-6667-1499-9
HARDCOVER ISBN: 978-1-6667-1500-2
EBOOK ISBN: 978-1-6667-1501-9

Cataloguing-in-Publication data:

Names: Finlan, Stephen, author.

Title: To unite the scattered children of God : hope for the spiritual uniting of humanity, from Isaiah to the present day / Stephen Finlan.

Description: Eugene, OR: Cascade Books, 2022 | Includes bibliographical references.

Identifiers: ISBN 978-1-6667-1499-9 (paperback) | ISBN 978-1-6667-1500-2 (hardcover) | ISBN 978-1-6667-1501-9 (ebook)

Subjects: LCSH: Christianity and other religions. | Theology of religions (Christian theology). | Christian unity. | Bible. Isaiah—Criticism, interpretation, etc.

Classification: BR127 .F50 2022 (paperback) | BR127 (ebook)

VERSION NUMBER 110322

Contents

Abbreviations

AD	Anno Domini
ANF	*The Ante-Nicene Fathers: Translations of the Writings of the Fathers down to A.D. 325*
ASV	American Standard Version
BC	Before Christ
BCE	Before Common Era
HCSB	Holman Christian Standard Bible
HTR	*Harvard Theological Review*
JTS	*Journal of Theological Studies*
LCL	Loeb Classical Library (Harvard University Press)
MT	Masoretic Text of the Hebrew Bible
NCV	New Century Version
NET	New English Translation
NKJV	New King James Version
NPNF 2	*A Select Library of the Nicene and Post-Nicene Fathers of the Christian Church*, Second Series
NRSV	New Revised Standard Version
NT	New Testament
OT	Old Testament
OTL	Old Testament Library (Westminster John Knox)

PG   *Patrologia Graeca*, multivolume work, ed. Jacques-Paul Migne.

PL   *Patrologia Latina*, multivolume work, ed. Jacques-Paul Migne.

PTM   Princeton Theological Monograph (Pickwick Press)

WJK   Westminster John Knox

WUNT   Wissenschaftliche Untersuchungen zum Neuen Testament (Mohr Siebeck)

Introduction

This book is largely motivated by what is seen in the subtitle: hope for the spiritual uniting of humanity. I have long been drawn to various statements in the Bible that speak either of drawing all peoples into the worship of the Lord, or of all people being invited into the kingdom of God as revealed by Jesus. I consider the theme of shared worship between Jews and Gentiles to be an aspect of the spiritual uniting of humanity. If the Gentiles are worshipping the God of Israel, and no longer waging war against Israel, this is a form of "spiritual uniting."

Jesus is the hope for the spiritual uniting of humanity. In his creative power resides the power of healing: spiritual healing and relationship healing, especially. He demonstrated for his apostles how to be open to Samaritans, Romans, and Canaanites (Luke 10:29–37; John 4:7–29, 40; Matt 8:5–13; 15:22–28). He tells his disciples to preach the gospel to all nations (Luke 24:47; Matt 24:14; 28:19), and to show compassion for the last and the least. He surprised people with the respect that he showed to women, children, and "foreigners." This love and respect changed people, and they change us whenever we practice them. The love and spirituality that he set in motion are meant to expand until they encompass the world.

There is a universalizing message in the OT as well, though it is outnumbered by nationalistic statements that speak of God favoring the people of Israel (as long as they are faithful to the covenant). Nevertheless, there was a widespread hope for a day when the nations would worship the God of Israel.

Throughout both parts of the Bible there is a strong universalizing trend. The fact that the universalizing texts in the OT are bucking the dominant trend makes their presence all the more remarkable and noticeable. The OT prophets were constantly universalizing the God-concept: "Many nations shall join themselves to the Lord on that day" (Zech 2:11).[1] "I am coming to gather all nations and tongues; and they shall come and shall see my glory" (Isa 66:18). "Are you not like the Ethiopians to me, O people of Israel? says the Lord. Did I not bring Israel up from the land of Egypt, and the Philistines from Caphtor and the Arameans from Kir?" (Amos 9:7). This is not a provincial God. But it is Jesus who systematically went beyond the nationalistic stage. He crafted a story about the goodness of a Samaritan, he rebuked his chief apostles when they wanted to call down fire upon the Samaritans, and when Jesus saw that a Roman centurion understood spiritual his authority, he said "I tell you, not even in Israel have I found such faith" (Luke 10:25–37; 9:54–55; 7:9).

He was not afraid to offend nationalistic pride. He rejected the nationalistic concept of the Messiah as the "son of David" (Matt 22:42–45; Mark 12:35, 37). On other occasions, he commended the goodness of a "foreigner" (Luke 17:18; Matt 15:28). He is truly the hope of uniting people "from all tribes and peoples and languages" (Rev 7:9). The teachings and the kindness of Jesus transform many people who come in contact with them. As the church father Irenaeus wrote, "He became as we are that we might become as he is."[2] This testifies to the transforming effect he is having upon the human race. Its cumulative effect may be slow, but it is inexorable.

Thus, I build my argument upon the teachings of the prophets, Jesus, Paul, and the fathers of the church. I will also build upon the philosophy of Teilhard de Chardin, who believed in the virtual inevitability of certain processes within the human race:

1. NRSV is the default Bible translation used throughout.
2. Irenaeus, *Against Heresies* 5, preface; ANF 1:526.

"constantly increasing unification, centration, and spiritualization
. . . [I]t would be easier to halt the revolution of the earth than
it would be to prevent the totalization of mankind."[3] "In virtue
of his position at the Omega of the World, Christ, we have seen,
represents the focus-point towards which and in which all things
converge."[4] Given the rise in nationalistic and ideological conflicts,
such a view seems unduly optimistic in the short run, but I wish to
affirm its validity in the long run. This is a biblical promise, after
all: "the earth will be filled with the knowledge of the glory of the
Lord, as the waters cover the sea" (Hab 2:14).

By "spiritualization," Teilhard means "the increasing predominance in the human layer of the reflective (or 'thought') over
automatic reactions and instinct."[5] I would say more: it represents
the internalization of spiritual qualities, the fruit of the spirit, the
marks of spiritual character. It is the ultimate goal, where "all of us
come to the unity of the faith and of the knowledge of the Son of
God, to maturity, to the measure of the full stature of Christ" (Eph
4:13). The human race is someday to be utterly transformed.

But let us begin with the universalizing trends within Jewish
literature, both biblical and postbiblical.

---

3. Teilhard de Chardin, "My Fundamental Vision," 181–82.

4. Teilhard de Chardin, *Let Me Explain*, 122.

5. Teilhard de Chardin, *Let Me Explain*, 183.

1

Attitudes in Isaiah
and Other Prophets

A universalizing stream flows through all parts of Isaiah, where the Gentiles will be drawn into God's family, though nationalistic elements are still present. Given the bellicose relations between Israel and its neighbors, it is not surprising that eschatological (end-time) hope would often involve throwing off a foreign yoke, and even subjugating foreign nations. But there are surprisingly many passages that speak of the Gentiles coming to worship the Lord.

First I want to mention why I accept the historical-critical division of Isaiah into three or four main periods of authorship, now designated First Isaiah, Second Isaiah, Third Isaiah, and the Isaiah Apocalypse. First Isaiah is full of autobiographical and geographical details, the names of Isaiah's allies and opponents, of Judean kings, and Assyrian kings. The events of these chapters occur from 740 BC to around 695 BC. Suddenly, in chapter 40, the writing style changes. There are no more historical narratives or autobiographies, only poetic oracles. The only reference to Assyria is to past oppression (52:4). The reigning power that is talked about is Chaldea. The Chaldeans were the ethnic group that ruled from Babylon and that conquered the Assyrians; Babylon is the name of a city and not of an ethnic group. God promises deliverance from the Chaldeans: "For your sake I will send to Babylon and break down all the bars, and the shouting of the Chaldeans will be turned to lamentation" (43:14). The Babylonian Empire will be laid low: "Sit in silence, and go into darkness, daughter Chaldea! For you shall no more be called the mistress of kingdoms" (47:5). The Jewish exiles are told to leave Babylon: "Go out from Babylon, flee from Chaldea" (48:20). The author is also aware of the up-and-coming king of the Persians, whom he mentions by name: "I have aroused Cyrus in righteousness, and I will make all his paths straight; he shall build my city and set my exiles free" (45:13). Cyrus did indeed release the Jews from exile in 538 BC, and supported their rebuilding of the Jerusalem temple (44:28). Scholars have concluded that chapters 40–55 were written near the end of the Babylonian exile, probably in the 530s BC.

The tone and form change again suddenly at chapter 56. The existence of a temple is assumed (56:6–7), which would be the Second Temple, established in 515 BC. Third Isaiah (chaps. 56–66) goes further than does Second Isaiah in his openness to the Gentiles. Finally, the Isaiah Apocalypse (chaps. 24–27) is recognized by most scholars as a late addition to the collection, with an apocalyptic content somewhat similar to chaps. 65–66. It is hard to date, but it makes sense to treat it after Third Isaiah.

Isaiah is a collection of writings that was augmented at certain times. It seems that certain enthusiastic readers of Isaiah expanded upon his themes, and some of their writings were incorporated into the collection. There are some themes that permeate all parts of Isaiah, although they are usually handled differently in the different parts. Let us look at the theme of Gentile inclusion in these parts, sequentially.

PEACE AND WORSHIP IN ISAIAH

First Isaiah

In chapter 2 comes the extraordinary passage where the Jerusalem temple becomes a focus for world peace.

> All the nations shall stream to it. Many peoples shall come and say, "Come, let us go up to the mountain of the Lord, to the house of the God of Jacob; that he may teach us his ways and that we may walk in his paths." For out of Zion shall go forth instruction, and the word of the Lord from Jerusalem. He shall judge between the nations, and shall arbitrate for many peoples; they shall beat their swords into ploughshares, and their spears into pruning-hooks; nation shall not lift up sword against nation, neither shall they learn war any more. (Isa 2:2–4)

This passage implies some kind of special role for the Jews, since it is at their temple that this will happen. But there is no suggestion that the claims of the other nations are illegitimate. Rather, God shall arbitrate fairly between the nations. Presumably Judah will be disarmed the same as all other nations, and all will benefit from world peace. It is a nearly unparalleled prophecy, although it is repeated nearly word for word in Micah 4:1–3, followed by a fascinating addition not found in Isaiah: "but they shall all sit under their own vines and under their own fig trees, and no one shall make them afraid; for the mouth of the Lord of hosts has spoken. For all the peoples walk, each in the name of its god, but we will walk in the name of the Lord our God for ever and ever" (Mic 4:4–5). The last verse, as we have it, seems to express a nationalistic bias: the other peoples will follow *their* gods, but *we* will follow *our* god. This bias runs counter to the drift of the preceding sentences, which is decidedly internationalistic and irenic.

The line "out of Zion shall go forth instruction" (Isa 2:3; Mic 4:2) is intriguing because the word for "instruction" is *torah*. Actually, "instruction" is a better translation for *torah* than is "law."[1] It

---

1. Jang, *Particularism and Universalism*, 158–59.

is this instruction that is sought by the Gentiles when they go "up to the mountain of the Lord . . . that he may teach us his ways" (Isa 2:3; Mic 4:2). Presumably the ways of peacemaking are being taught, since both passages immediately move into the swords-into-ploughshares sentence.

Isaiah 2 shows Zion (shorthand for Jerusalem) functioning no longer as a national capital, but as a world capital, even "the world governmental centre."[2] It is the place from which YHWH himself will rule the nations and instruct them. As we continue to read through all parts of Isaiah, we will see that "Zion" has a dual role. Besides standing as a symbolic name for Jerusalem, and for Judah as a whole, it also becomes the center to which the Gentiles are drawn, and from which YHWH will rule, although nowhere so explicitly as in chapter 2.

Inclusion of the Gentiles is a theme that occurs repeatedly in Isaiah, often in passages that move back and forth between nationalism and universalism. Isaiah 9 has an inclusive theme, showing up in the first verse: "he will make glorious the way of the sea, the land beyond the Jordan, Galilee of the nations." This seems to be emphasizing the Gentiles who neighbored Galilee, or possibly dwelt next to Jews *in* Galilee. The nationalist theme appears in the rest of this passage. "The rod of their oppressor" will be broken (9:4), which implies a foreign oppressor. The messianic figure who will save them will occupy "the throne of David . . . He will establish and uphold it with justice and righteousness" (9:7). The "Galilee" passage is quoted in Matthew 4. Jesus made his "home in Capernaum . . . so that what had been spoken through the prophet Isaiah might be fulfilled" (Matt 4:13–14). Isaiah 9 is then quoted in Matthew 4:15–16.

One of the most remarkable, and most neglected, of the promises of harmony occurs in Isaiah 11. Isaiah speaks of a messianic figure who will be endowed with a sevenfold spirit: "The spirit of the Lord shall rest on him, the spirit of wisdom and understanding, the spirit of counsel and might, the spirit of knowledge and the fear of the Lord" (11:2). He will "decide with equity for the meek of

---

2. Jang, *Particularism and Universalism*, 174.

the earth," and "with the breath of his lips he shall kill the wicked" (11:4), but these groups (the "meek" and the "wicked") are not defined in national terms. This ruler will usher in a new age, where the typical dangers of the natural world will not threaten anymore: "the leopard shall lie down with the kid" and no one will be hurt, "for the earth will be full of the knowledge of the Lord as the waters cover the sea" (Isa 11:6, 9). The whole world will be changed, and the world will come to know God. Gentiles will come to inquire of the Jews about God: "On that day the root of Jesse shall stand as a signal to the peoples; the nations shall inquire of him" (11:10).

After this vision of a changed world, where Gentiles will inquire about God, there follows a nationalistic element: the refugees, the "outcasts of Israel" will be summoned back from Assyria, Egypt, Ethiopia, and other lands (11:11–12). Even this focus on Israel at the end does not undo the optimistic promise of the whole world being filled with the knowledge of the Lord (11:9).

That verse is repeated almost word for word in the sixth-century prophet Habakkuk, but with "of the glory" added: "the earth will be filled with the knowledge of the glory of the Lord, as the waters cover the sea" (2:14). This remarkable passage is mostly neglected in subsequent interpretation, both by the authors of the New Testament and by the church fathers. Habakkuk envisions the oppressive Babylonian empire being overthrown (2:8), and then, in contrast, people throughout the world coming to know the glory of Lord. Consequently, God's will is done on earth. In Isaiah 11, the promise comes as part of a prophecy of the messianic kingdom, a transformed world where "the wolf shall live with the lamb" (11:6), where there will be justice and gentleness everywhere. In Isaiah, the promise fits in with the other extraordinary transformations envisioned for the world. In Habakkuk 2, the promise comes as a stark contrast to the injustice imposed by an oppressive empire (Chaldea). The passage does not fit so well in Habakkuk as in the earlier prophet First Isaiah. Habakkuk probably borrowed and reworked the saying.

The next Isaiah passage reinforces the teaching that God will be made known to the nations. Readers are promised that "with joy you will draw water from the wells of salvation" (Isa 12:3). This is directed at all humanity. It is to be "ma[d]e known . . . among the nations" (12:4), and is to be proclaimed "in all the earth" (12:5). The glory of God will be world-renowned.

One of the most remarkable passages is one that speaks of the worship of YHWH taking place in Egypt, and God even rescuing the Egyptians if anyone oppresses them: "On that day there will be an altar to the Lord in the center of the land of Egypt, and a pillar to the Lord at its border. It will be a sign and a witness to the Lord of hosts in the land of Egypt; when they cry to the Lord because of oppressors, he will send them a savior, and will defend and deliver them. The Lord will make himself known to the Egyptians; and the Egyptians will know the Lord on that day" (Isa 19:19–21). Isaiah also foresees an equality of status between Egypt, Assyria, and Israel. "The Egyptians will worship with the Assyrians. On that day Israel will be the third with Egypt and Assyria, a blessing in the midst of the earth, whom the Lord of hosts has blessed, saying, 'Blessed be Egypt my people, and Assyria the work of my hands, and Israel my heritage'" (19:23–25). It is extraordinary to see similar affectionate language used for Egypt and Assyria as is used for Israel. All three will be worshiping together, and all three are beloved by God. Egypt and Assyria were the two superpowers of the day, and tended to treat Israel as a pawn or as an irritant, to be used or to be crushed. Here all three are to be allies and fellow worshipers. There will even be an altar to the Lord in the center of Egypt.

There is a strong loyalty to Jerusalem and to Judah in First Isaiah, including a promise that the Lord would rescue Jerusalem from the siege that Sennacherib the Assyrian placed upon Jerusalem in 701 BC. "The Lord of hosts will protect Jerusalem . . . The Assyrian shall fall by a sword, not of mortals" (31:5, 8). Indeed, it seems Jerusalem was astonishingly rescued, possibly by bubonic plague spreading in the Assyrian army (described by Herodotus as mice eating away the soldiers' scabbards, *History* 2.141; described as the angel of the Lord striking down 185,000 Assyrian soldiers overnight in 1 Kings 19:35).

In summary, First Isaiah has a number of extraordinary eschatological passages of a splendid optimistic nature, hopes for world peace (chapter 2), for a just kingdom including even "Galilee of the nations" (chapter 9), for the worship of the God of Israel by Egypt and Assyria, "my people" and "the work of my hands," respectively (chapter 19), for a transformation of the whole world which would bring equity to the meek of the earth (chapter 11), and for salvation that will be known in all the world (chapter 12). The messianic visions are an essential part of Isaiah's message. There will come a day when "the nations shall inquire of him" (11:10), and he will "decide with equity for the meek of the earth" (11:4).

Second Isaiah

Second Isaiah spends considerable time comforting the Jewish people and promising that they will be vindicated and restored, and also that they will become teachers of the Gentiles. This Isaiah has an extraordinary optimism about the potential spiritual responsiveness of the Gentiles: "Here is my servant . . . he will bring forth justice to the nations . . . I have given you as a covenant to the people, a light to the nations, to open the eyes that are blind, to bring out the prisoners from the dungeon, from the prison those who sit in darkness" (Isa 42:1, 6–7). Gentile eyes will be opened. The Jews will be teachers who will draw the Gentiles in; they are "a light to the nations" (Isa 42:6). Later in that oracle, Gentiles shall be praising God in the coastlands, the desert, and the cities (Isa 42:10–12). The author simultaneously uplifts the hopes of the Jews for their own vindication and rescue, and promises a new connection to the Gentiles.

In the very first chapter of Second Isaiah, the universalizing message is heard: "the glory of the Lord shall be revealed, and all people shall see it together" (40:5). The supremacy of God over the whole human race is made clear: "The Lord is the everlasting God, the Creator of the ends of the earth" (40:28).

The notion of the Jews teaching the Gentiles about the one God is repeated in chapter 49. God says, in effect, it's not enough "that you should be my servant to raise up the tribes of Jacob and to restore the survivors of Israel; I will give you as a light to the nations, that my salvation may reach to the end of the earth. . . . Kings shall see and stand up, princes, and they shall prostrate themselves, because of the Lord, who is faithful, the Holy One of Israel, who has chosen you" (Isa 49:6–7). The saving influence of believers in the God of Israel is meant to extend far beyond Israel, to be a light for all the other peoples. But the theme of Jewish supremacy persists; the kings who prostrate themselves before the Holy One of Israel will know that the deity has chosen the Jews.

The nations will return the Jewish exiles whom they hold: "I will soon lift up my hand to the nations, and raise my signal to the peoples; and they shall bring your sons in their bosom, and your daughters shall be carried on their shoulders" (49:22). Along with this, they will have to abase themselves to the Jews: "With their faces to the ground they shall bow down to you, and lick the dust of your feet" (49:23). Even some statements about the world turning to YHWH present it as a vindication of Israel: "The Lord has bared his holy arm before the eyes of all the nations; and all the ends of the earth shall see the salvation of our God" (52:10).

From the Jews they will learn about God, and they will worship together with the Jews, but also submit themselves to the Jews. "The Sabeans, tall of stature, shall come over to you and be yours, they shall follow you; they shall come over in chains and bow down to you. They will make supplication to you, saying, 'God is with you alone, and there is no other; there is no god besides him'" (Isa 45:14). Jewish supremacy is part of the vision of international peace and shared worship: "your descendants will possess the nations" (54:3).

God's message and method will rule the nations: "A teaching will go out from me, and my justice for a light to the peoples . . . my salvation has gone out and my arms will rule the peoples; the coastlands wait for me, and for my arm they hope" (Isa 51:4–5).[3] Both God's power (his "arms") and his justice will prevail over the nations, and they will learn to hope in him. Exactly *how* the power

3. See Ramelli, *Larger Hope?*, 9–10.

of God will be asserted over the nations is not clear, but the end result is that they will come to worship the Lord. They will be convinced by the Jewish teaching. "Let all the nations gather together, and let the peoples assemble. . . . Let them bring their witnesses to justify them, and let them hear and say, 'It is true'" (43:9). "Turn to me and be saved, all the ends of the earth!" (Isa 45:22).

Another passage that involves the nations acknowledging the God of Israel is 52:10: "The Lord has bared his holy arm before the eyes of all the nations; and all the ends of the earth shall see the salvation of our God." There is also a tone of Israelite superiority in this promise: "you shall call nations that you do not know, and nations that do not know you shall run to you, because of the Lord your God, the Holy One of Israel, for he has glorified you" (55:5). Jews will become the religious teachers of the nations. I don't think this was only futuristic; some of this was already happening in Second Isaiah's own experience. It is hard to imagine such extravagant and repeated hopes without at least some basis in personal experience. The prophet got through to some Gentiles.

Third Isaiah

Third Isaiah is the most universalizing of the Isaianic authors. One remarkable passage is in Isaiah 56.

> Do not let the foreigner joined to the Lord say, "The Lord will surely separate me from his people" . . . The foreigners will who join themselves to the Lord, to minister to him, to love the name of the Lord, and to be his servants . . . these I will bring to my holy mountain, and make them joyful in my house of prayer; their burnt-offerings and their sacrifices will be accepted on my altar; for my house shall be called a house of prayer for all peoples. (56:3, 6–7)

Of course, that last line is used by Jesus in his criticism and "cleansing" of the temple (Mark 11:17). Third Isaiah does not use the term "Zion" in this passage, but does refer to "my holy mountain" (56:7). The author picks up some themes from the peace passage in Isaiah 2, developing some of them much further. Foreigners will not come just to be taught, but they will be active participants in temple worship; God will honor them and "make them joyful." The temple is really *for* them, as well as for Israel. "Thus says the Lord God, who gathers the outcasts of Israel, I will gather others to them besides those already gathered" (56:8). Isaiah 56 shatters not only the national exclusivity of Jews over against Gentiles, it also eliminates the privilege of the Levites of being the only ones to serve in the temple. This is one of the most socially radical passages in the Hebrew Bible.

It seems that a new epoch has dawned in Jewish religion, made possible by the collapse of nationalistic hopes in the Babylonian exile, directed by Second Isaiah's shaping of hope into more spiritual categories and with a notion of mission to the nations, and culminating in Third Isaiah's daring reversal of the law's exclusivism. Third Isaiah is bold and energetic, evidently believing that the written prophetic word really carries weight. He seems to have a realized eschatology: the promises about the end times are happening *now* in the prophet's time. End-time events occur now, whenever Jews use the new scale of values, and allow devout Gentiles into the community.

Chapter 60 has universalizing lines, but surrounded by nationalistic content. "Nations shall come to your light" (Isa 60:3). This is followed by promises that the nations will come to the Jews, bearing gifts (60:6, 11), and carrying Jewish exiles with them (60:4, 9). The other nations will be like servants: "Foreigners shall build up your walls, and their kings shall minister to you . . . You shall suck the milk of nations" (60:10, 16). "The descendants of those who oppressed you shall come bending low to you" (60:14). Any "kingdom that will not serve you shall perish" (60:12). But their worship will be acceptable: "All the flocks of Kedar shall be gathered to you, the rams of Nebaioth shall minister to you; they shall be acceptable on my altar" (60:7).

One of the most universalizing passages is also one that was strangely neglected in later (rabbinic and Christian) interpretation: "as the earth brings forth its shoots, and as a garden causes what is sown in it to spring up, so the Lord God will cause righteousness and praise to spring up before all the nations" (Isa 61:11).

Isaiah 65 speaks of a "new heavens and a new earth" (65:17), with a promise of a transformed world similar to Isaiah 11's: "No more shall the sound of weeping be heard in [Jerusalem], or the cry of distress. No more shall there be in it an infant that lives but a few days, or an old person who does not live out a lifetime . . . The wolf and the lamb shall feed together, the lion shall eat straw like the ox" (Isa 65:19–20, 25). New creation is a major theme in Isaiah, and it continues, in different ways, in the New Testament.

The last chapter in Isaiah is highly universalizing, and contains some anti-ritual passages, as Isaiah 1 had done: "Whoever slaughters an ox is like one who kills a human being; whoever sacrifices a lamb, like one who breaks a dog's neck" (66:3). Isaiah 66:18–23 contains some of the most universalistic material in the OT: "I am coming to gather all nations and tongues; and they shall come and shall see my glory" (66:18). The advocacy of missionary outreach to the Gentiles is even greater than it was in Second Isaiah; in fact, representatives of the nations will themselves become missionaries to the nations: "I will set a sign among them. From them I will send survivors to the nations, to Tarshish, Put, and Lud—which draw the bow—to Tubal and Javan, to the coastlands far away that have not heard of my fame or seen my glory; and they shall declare my glory among the nations . . . And I will also take some of them as priests and as Levites" (66:19, 21). Remarkably, "foreigners will be chosen as priests and Levites, a universal priesthood available to a new community."[4] It is a worldwide community. God is working on the whole human race: "All flesh shall come to worship before me, says the Lord" (66:23). The astounding implication is that the nations that come to believe in YHWH will no longer require the mediating service of Israel.

This is "corrected" in vv. 20–22, where the primacy of Israel is asserted, and where the foreigners carry the Jews back to Judah.[5] Westermann felt that there was "an abrupt confrontation

4. Jang, *Particularism and Universalism*, 181–82.
5. Westermann, *Isaiah 40–66*, 423, 427.

between universalism and particularism" in Isaiah 66, which is never harmonized.[6] But the final canonical shape of the material represents at least a peaceful coexistence between the two viewpoints. The receivers of the text were able to *consider* it sufficiently harmonized. The nations are saved and they are not said to be subservient. However, the conservative viewpoint has the last word; in v. 24 "the people who have rebelled against me" (probably uncooperative Gentiles) are subjected to burning.

The Isaiah Apocalypse

Besides Third Isaiah, there is what appears to be a late addition to Isaiah, often called the "Isaiah Apocalypse" (chaps. 24–27). Blenkinsopp says these chapters probably belong to the latest phases of the editing and collecting of the book of Isaiah, a phase that took on an apocalyptic character.[7] An intriguing eschatological passage occurs in chapter 24: "On that day the Lord will punish the host of heaven in heaven, and on earth the kings of the earth. They will be gathered together like prisoners in a pit; they will be shut up in a prison, and after many days they will be punished" (24:21–22). This joins together a promised punishment of the host of heaven and of earthly kings. It calls to mind later traditions about a rebellion in heaven (Rev 12:3–4, 7), and the binding of Satan (Rev 20:2–3), or the binding of Asael and Shemihazah in *First Enoch* (1 *En* 10:4, 11–14). Although those details are not explicit in this passage, there are significant parallels: a heavenly host who need to be punished, and who will be thrown into a pit and bound for many days. The events are of cosmic importance: "Then the moon will be abashed, and the sun ashamed; for the Lord of hosts will reign on Mount Zion and in Jerusalem" (Isa 24:23).

It is not clear what is supposed to happen afterward, but the next chapter does give us a very significant passage about the whole human race: "On this mountain the Lord of hosts will make

6. Westermann, *Isaiah 40–66*, 423.

7. Blenkinsopp, *Opening the Sealed Book*, 16, 18.

for all peoples a feast of rich food, a feast of well-matured wines, of rich food filled with marrow, of well-matured wines strained clear. And he will destroy on this mountain the shroud that is cast over all peoples, the sheet that is spread over all nations; he will swallow up death for ever. Then the Lord God will wipe away the tears from all faces, and the disgrace of his people he will take away from all the earth" (Isa 25:6–8). What a remarkable promise regarding "all peoples" and "all faces." What is that shroud or sheet? Is it death? Death certainly casts a pall over us. The next line implies that this is the topic, since it says "he will swallow up death for ever" (25:8). However, I think it could be the *fear* of death that shrouds human life. Worry and dread of death so pervade our lives. Or is the shroud *sorrow*? That might be implied by the following line where "the Lord God will wipe away tears from all faces" (25:8). The shroud of sorrow will someday be relieved. Or maybe it is shame and disgrace. The author says "the disgrace of his people he will take away from all the earth" (25:8). Shame can be like a shroud that blocks people from living fully, since they feel reduced and disgraced in the sight of others. They relive the shaming experience, and are oppressed by it over and over. One of these things, or *all* of these things—death, fear, sorrow, or shame—are the shroud that shall be removed from all the nations.

This rings true. Doesn't it seem that the minds of people are shrouded, that so many lives are stifled somehow by fear or sorrow or shame? How accurate is the description in Isaiah! Now think of a spiritual gift that feels like the *lifting* of a shroud, a rediscovery of freedom and a restoration of the joy of living. If the shroud has been lifted for you, if you have been saved by faith and the light of love has poured in, what rejoicing you have had!

Now, is this removal of the shroud something that God will do, something that we humans will do, or something that God and humans must cooperate in doing? I think it has to be the latter. This is where Isaiah does not say enough. It is Christ's teaching about reflecting God's love and spreading it to others that completes the story for us. We have to build communities of love based on recognition of the love of God. When we do this kingdom work, we are contributing to the day when all tears will be dried, when the shroud that is over the human race will be removed, when faith, hope, and love will be the dominant characteristics that shape human life. The late contributor to the Isaiah collection gives it an apocalyptic frame, having God do all the transformative work. Second and Third Isaiah have more to say about human cooperation in the Lord's transformative work: Jews acting as a light to the Gentiles (42:6; 49:6), foreigners ministering to the Lord (56:6), Jews calling nations to them (55:5).

The Isaiah Apocalypse has some more passages that are useful for our thesis. "For when your judgments are in the earth, the inhabitants of the world learn righteousness" (26:9). The "world" is the focus here. This recalls passages from the other parts of Isaiah that speak of the Gentiles learning about the Lord. There is also a rare passage about an afterlife: "Your dead shall live, their corpses shall rise. O dwellers in the dust, awake and sing for joy! For your dew is a radiant dew, and the earth will give birth to those long dead" (26:19).

Of course, the nationalist emphasis is also present. One of the promises is that the nations that war against Judah will be defeated: "the multitude of all the nations that fight against Ariel, all that fight against her and her stronghold, and who distress her, shall be like a dream, a vision of the night" (29:7).

Summarizing the Isaiahs

What can be said, in summary, about Isaiah? Statements about the Gentiles worshipping the Lord, being friends with the Jews, and even being worthy to serve in the temple are unexpected. But they occur often enough that we have to recognize that eschatological universalism is a major theme throughout Isaiah.

And yet, "much of the universalism derives from assumptions of a religio-moral superiority based on the possession of the divinely revealed law."[8] Another trenchant observation is this

8. Robinson, *Jesus and the Religions*, 50.

one: "While much of Isa. 60–2, as well as Isa. 59:15b–20, 63:1–6, 66:12, 16, conveys a hostile standpoint vis-à-vis the Gentiles, the material in Isa. 56:1–8 and 66:18–21 reflects a more inclusive perspective. . . . Zech. 2:11, 8:22, 14:16–21, and Mal. 1:11 speak of the participation of the Gentiles in the worship of YHWH. . . . The Gentiles have but two choices: military annihilation or acceptance of an active participation in the Israelite religion."[9]

Tiemeyer perceives a strong national emphasis, but does grant that a "more inclusive perspective" exists. I would put more attention on the inclusive perspective than she does. It continues to recur throughout Isaiah, and its very counterintuitive nature commands attention. "I am coming to gather all nations and tongues. . . . All flesh shall come to worship before me, says the Lord" (Isa 66:18, 23). This is no minor opinion, but a major shift in emphasis from nationalism. It entails a new friendship between peoples formerly hostile to each other. We saw this in other chapters, too. Egypt, Assyria, and Israel will all be embraced by God (19:23–25). Foreigners will "love the name of the Lord" (56:6). Such transformations would be miraculous, and they are affirmed in at least four different authorial levels in Isaiah, in authors stretching from the eighth to the fifth or fourth centuries BC (First Isaiah, Second Isaiah, Third Isaiah, the Isaiah Apocalypse).

Tiemeyer says that these positive passages often occur near the end of a major section, "are not fully integrated into the surrounding material," and that the negative statements "stand at loggerheads with the 'positive' ones."[10] Tiemeyer posits that the negative and positive statements were inserted by different editors of the Isaiah collection.[11] There are exceptions to her characterization. Isaiah 2 is not at the end of any major section, nor are Isaiah 19 or 25. It may be that different editors inserted negative and positive comments about the Gentiles, but the fact is that both kinds of passages were accepted into the text as we have it, and the

---

9. Tiemeyer, "Death or Conversion," 1.

10. Tiemeyer, "Death or Conversion," 2.

11. Tiemeyer, "Death or Conversion," 2.

positive passages have a unique and astonishing message that does not fit with the nationalistic viewpoint.

To some extent, the prophetic statements could be seen as a development from the early promise to Abraham that "in you all the families of the earth shall be blessed . . . all the nations of the earth shall be blessed in him" (Gen 12:3; 18:18; cf. 22:18). The blessings to Abraham were also understood to be a blessing to all of humanity. Genesis 12:3 is quoted by Peter in one of his early sermons in Acts (3:25). Paul builds his case of a universal gospel upon the promise of all nations being blessed through Abraham (Gal 3:8).

THE BOOK OF ZECHARIAH

The book of Zechariah parallels the book of Isaiah in two important ways: many of the same universalizing themes occur in both collections, and both collections seem to fall into three main sections (Zechariah into chaps 1–8, 9–11, and 12–14). A hope that occurs near the beginning of Zechariah ("Many nations shall join themselves to the Lord on that day, and shall be my people; and I will dwell in your midst," 2:11 [2:15 MT[12]]) recurs near the end of First Zechariah ("the inhabitants of one city shall go to another, saying, 'Come, let us go to entreat the favor of the Lord, and to seek the Lord of hosts; I myself am going.' . . . Many peoples and strong nations shall come to seek the Lord of hosts in Jerusalem, and to entreat the favor of the Lord," 8:21–22). Even powerful nations will come to Jerusalem to learn about God and seek his favor. This implies peace between Israel and these nations. In fact, the daily lives of Jews will contribute to peace. As Zechariah says, "Speak the truth to one another, render in your gates judgments that are true and make for peace" (Zech 8:16). Truthfulness, justice, and peace work together.

Earlier in the book there is a passage where an angel tells Zechariah what God's message to Zerubbabel, the ruler of

12. The Masoretic Text, the standard Jewish text of the Hebrew Bible, sometimes has different verse numbering than the standard English translations.

Jerusalem, is: "Not by might, nor by power, but by my spirit, says the Lord of hosts" (4:6). This anti-militaristic principle recurs throughout Zechariah.

We see it taken further in Second Zechariah in an extraordinary prophecy of a peace Messiah: "Shout aloud, O daughter Jerusalem! Lo, your king comes to you; triumphant and victorious is he, humble and riding on a donkey, on a colt, the foal of a donkey. He will cut off the chariot from Ephraim and the warhorse from Jerusalem; and the battle-bow shall be cut off, and he shall command peace to the nations" (Zech 9:9–10). No wonder that Jesus deliberately chose to dramatically enact this prophecy when he rode into Jerusalem on a donkey (Mark 11:1–7; John 12:14–16), affirming his commitment to nonviolence.

The end of Third Zechariah contains an important passage. "Then all who survive of the nations that have come against Jerusalem shall go up year by year to worship the King, the Lord of hosts, and to keep the festival of booths" (14:16). The physical and moral landscape is re-formed, and "the Lord shall become king over the whole earth" (14:9). Holiness shall be redefined, no longer confined solely to priestly objects: "On that day there shall be inscribed on the bells of the horses, 'Holy to the Lord.' And the cooking-pots in the house of the Lord shall be as holy as the bowls in front of the altar; and every cooking-pot in Jerusalem and Judah shall be sacred to the Lord of hosts" (Zech 14:20–21). In an eschatological vision, the boundary between holiness and unholiness can come down, and also the boundary between Jews and Gentiles.

In some prophets, there is theology that could be called reactionary, deliberately rejecting or reversing the peace prophecies of Isaiah and Zechariah. Joel, for instance, speaks of nations beating "your ploughshares into swords and your pruning-hooks into spears" and then waging war against Judah (3:10, 12). But the Lord will be a refuge for his people, and strangers will never pass through Jerusalem again (3:16–17). The book ends with an ominous promise: "I will avenge their blood, and I will not clear the guilty, for the Lord dwells in Zion" (3:21). Clearly, there is an ongoing debate within the prophetic collections about this issue.

The final prophetic book affirms the international fame of the Lord: "from the rising of the sun to its setting my name is great among the nations, and in every place incense is offered to my name, and a pure offering; for my name is great among the nations" (Mal 1:11). This affirms that YHWH will receive respect throughout the world.

UNIVERSALISM IN THE PSALMS AND OTHER BOOKS

The principle of universal worship continues in the Psalms: "all the families of the nations shall worship before him" (22:27). "Peoples gather together, and kingdoms, to worship the Lord" (102:22).

One of the most intense lines in the psalms is this one: "He makes wars cease to the end of the earth; he breaks the bow, and shatters the spear; he burns the shields with fire. 'Be still, and know that I am God! I am exalted among the nations, I am exalted in the earth'" (46:9–10). Apparently, God will be exalted and acknowledged worldwide when he breaks the battle bows of all nations and brings an end to war.

God even guides the nations: "Let the nations be glad and sing for joy, for you judge the peoples with equity and guide the nations upon earth" (67:4). Of course, the nationalism is still present in many psalms: "Ask of me, and I will make the nations your heritage, and the ends of the earth your possession. You shall break them with a rod of iron" (2:8–9); "May all kings fall down before him, all nations give him service" (72:11). The antecedent of "him" is the Davidic king: "Give the king your justice, O God" (72:1). Still, the nations themselves will be blessed: "May all nations be blessed in him" (72:17). All of this fits within the notion that "God is the king of all the earth . . . God is king over the nations" (47:7–8).

Even for the individual, there is a promise: "The Lord will fulfill his purpose for me" (Ps 138:8).

Psalm 96 reaffirms the supremacy of God over the earth (96:7–10). Further, "he will judge the world with righteousness" (96:13). This continues in the following psalms. "You, O Lord, are most high over all the earth" (97:9). "All the ends of the earth have seen the victory of our God" (98:3). "He is exalted over all the peoples" (99:2).

Later books of the Bible, specifically of the Septuagint, reiterated the idea of Gentiles converting to the worship of the God of Israel. "Then the nations in the whole world will all be converted and worship God in truth. They will all abandon their idols, which deceitfully have led them into their error; and in righteousness they will praise the eternal God" (Tobit 14:6–7).[13]

UNIVERSALISM IN JUDAISM

Malka Simkovich has written a masterful book on an important universalizing stream within Judaism, especially Hellenistic Judaism. She offers a definition: "Universalist literature presumes that all people, regardless of religion, have access to a relationship with the Israelite God and the benefits which He promises to those loyal to Him, without demanding that they convert or participate in the Jewish community *as a Jew*."[14] In her understanding, a truly universalist viewpoint does not retain the idea of the "subjugation of the nations," but rather sees "all of humankind standing on an equal footing in relation to the One True God."[15] Simkovich discerns two types of universalistic literature emerging in the Jewish tradition: first, "Universalized Worship invites all of humankind to worship the One True God without expectation that they will assimilate into the Jewish covenantal community . . . ethnic boundaries . . . remain intact"; the second type, "which I call Ethical Universalism, also invites all of humankind to worship the One True God. In this model, the distinctive aspects of Judaism are

---

13. Donaldson, *Judaism and the Gentiles*, 44.

14. Simkovich, *Making of Jewish Universalism*, xviii–xix.

15. Simkovich, *Making of Jewish Universalism*, xx.

dissolved . . . ethnic boundaries . . . fall to the wayside."[16] This second type is strongly influenced by Stoic thought. Previous studies of this subject have been distorted, in her view, by putting a focus on conversion, "which is not a universalist concept."[17]

Universalistic Worship is one of the four models for relations between Jews and non-Jews that she finds in the eschatology of the biblical prophets. The other three models are "Israel as Subjugators, Israel as Standard-Bearers, [and] Naturalized Nations."[18] In the first, "Israel dominates its former enemies . . . In the Israel as Standard-Bearers model, Zion functions as a light for all of humankind, and the nations remain separate from one another . . . In the Naturalized Nations model, the foreign nations assimilate into the Israelite covenant and participate in the Israelite community as full members."[19] As one proceeds through these three types to the later types, Universalized Worship and the postbiblical model of Ethical Universalism, one finds that references to the exodus, to Sinai, and to Sabbath and dietary regulations diminish or disappear altogether. Examples of Ethical Universalist texts written from the second century BCE to the first century CE include the Sentences of Pseudo-Phocylides and the Third Sibylline Oracle, "probably written within the Alexandrian Jewish community."[20] Philo of Alexandria appropriates some Stoic ideas, but she says he is not a universalist, since he highlights "the separateness of Judaism as a distinct religion, but also its superiority to Greek culture."[21] However, Stoic thinking seems to be reflected in his statement that "A man who is obedient to the law, being, by so doing, a citizen of the world, arranges his actions with reference to the intention of nature."[22]

---

16. Simkovich, *Making of Jewish Universalism*, xxii.
17. Simkovich, *Making of Jewish Universalism*, xxiii.
18. Simkovich, *Making of Jewish Universalism*, xxiv.
19. Simkovich, *Making of Jewish Universalism*, xxiv.
20. Simkovich, *Making of Jewish Universalism*, xxvi.
21. Simkovich, *Making of Jewish Universalism*, xxvi.
22. Philo of Alexandria, *On the Creation* 3; *Works of Philo*, 3.

Particular authors can express more than one of these models of thought. "The universalist and particularist aspects of Early Jewish literature are not representative of two oppositional streams of thought."[23] Both viewpoints can be found, for instance, in Zechariah 14 and in Third Isaiah.

The famous war-no-more passage in Isaiah 2:2–4 and Micah 4:1–5 is an example of the Israel as Standard-Bearers model, in which foreign nations acknowledge the God of Israel, but there is no mention of their participation in Israelite cultic worship, which would have entailed a drastic social change.[24] Simkovich argues that only the Standard-Bearer model is widely present within Second Isaiah, but not actual universalism, "since these passages do not suggest that all of humankind may equally participate in an ongoing covenantal relationship . . . or worshipping God in an ongoing way as non-Israelites."[25] I think her reading may be a little too strict here. If God's salvation is reaching "to the end of the earth" (49:6), that implies that the people who are saved are worshipping. If God is not giving up his praise to idols (42:8), right after speaking of giving the Servant as a "light to the nations" (42:6), that implies that the nations are giving praise to God rather than idols, and covenant is explicitly mentioned, although it is applied to the Servant and not to the nations. Still, I think these are universalizing passages. I find that Isaiah 42:6–7—"I have given you as a covenant to the people, a light to the nations, to open the eyes that are blind, to bring out the prisoners from the dungeon"—implies that Gentile eyes are opened and Gentile prisoners released.

Simkovich sees the Naturalized Nations model, in which foreign nations are "absorbed into the Israelite community," in Zechariah 2:10–17 MT (2:6–13 in NRSV).[26] "Many nations shall join themselves to the Lord on that day, and shall be my people; and I will dwell in your midst" (Zech 2:11, v. 15 in the MT). Esther contains a good example of the Naturalized Nations model, a

23. Simkovich, *Making of Jewish Universalism*, 141.
24. Simkovich, *Making of Jewish Universalism*, 12.
25. Simkovich, *Making of Jewish Universalism*, 16.
26. Simkovich, *Making of Jewish Universalism*, 16.

theme that existed in the Hebrew but was heightened in the Greek translation of Esther. In both versions, many Gentile nations become Jewish at the end, "because the fear of the Jews had fallen upon them" (Esth 8:17).[27]

It may be that some prophets did not make the sharp distinction between Naturalized Nations and Universalized Worship that Simkovich makes. In both those models, Gentiles come to worship the God of Israel. Some biblical authors may have focused on that shared worship, and not have reasoned out whether or not the Gentiles will be giving up their national identities.

Simkovich sees Isaiah 56 and 66 as the clearest biblical examples of Universalized Worship. In Isaiah 56:1, 8, God gathers "those foreigners who observe the Sabbath" and accepts their sacrifices; they are "welcomed into the covenantal community,"[28] yet they retain their identity as separate "peoples" (56:7). In Isaiah 66:18–24, God's Holy Mount is again seen "as the center of the nations' worship," while in 66:22 "the Judeans' name will be permanently preserved," meaning that the nations are not absorbed into Judah.[29] Like Isaiah 66, Zechariah 14 predicts punishment for those who do not worship God in Jerusalem; these threats do not undermine the presence of universalism in these passages; it only means "all nations have the same choice as the Israelites do, to either enter into this covenant or to risk divine wrath."[30]

She says, "the Universalized Worship model was developed in the post-exilic period, when Jews living under the newly expanded Persian Empire were optimistic that they were embarking on a period that would be characterized by religious freedom and the universal acknowledgment of the One True God."[31]

In the centuries preceding Jesus, there were many mentions of people called "God-fearers." The God-fearers were Gentiles who practiced some Jewish customs but probably did not constitute

27. Simkovich, *Making of Jewish Universalism*, 59.
28. Simkovich, *Making of Jewish Universalism*, 28–29.
29. Simkovich, *Making of Jewish Universalism*, 33.
30. Simkovich, *Making of Jewish Universalism*, 36.
31. Simkovich, *Making of Jewish Universalism*, 41.

a distinct group.[32] Three Jewish works composed from 250 to around 140 BC perpetuate the Universalized Worship model with frequent reference to God-fearers. Tobit says "the nations in the whole world will all be converted [*epistrépsousin*] and will worship [*phobeisthai*] God in truth. They will all abandon their idols" (14:6). Simkovich thinks *epistrépsousin* would more accurately be translated "will turn toward," which contributes to her conclusion that the nations are not naturalized, but keep their separate national identities, and "worship God without converting into the Jewish faith."[33] Joseph and Asenath is a story about Joseph and his Egyptian wife who "beseeches" and attaches herself to the Most High.[34] The Letter of Aristeas describes the Ptolemaic sponsorship of the Septuagint, the translation of the Hebrew Bible into Greek that took place largely from 283 to 246 BC. The Letter of Aristeas states "that Jews and Gentiles worship the same God," which "implies that all of humankind are united with one another in common worship."[35]

In the Letter of Aristeas, Simkovich sees the influence of Stoic thinking. Stoicism was a highly influential Greek philosophy that believed in "*homónoia*, the unity of humankind."[36] The concept lent itself to religious synthesis. "If the Greeks were engaged with the concept of world unity and *homónoia* between the fourth and first centuries BCE, it is no great surprise that the topic of universal love infiltrated Jewish literature."[37]

In the important Jewish philosopher Philo of Alexandria there are both universalist and particularist elements present. He writes of God, "Whom all Greeks and barbarians unanimously acknowledge, the supreme Father of gods and men and the Maker of the whole universe . . . it was the duty of all men to cleave to Him."[38]

---

32. Simkovich, *Making of Jewish Universalism*, 69.

33. Simkovich, *Making of Jewish Universalism*, 70–71.

34. Simkovich, *Making of Jewish Universalism*, 73.

35. Simkovich, *Making of Jewish Universalism*, 75–76.

36. Simkovich, *Making of Jewish Universalism*, 76.

37. Simkovich, *Making of Jewish Universalism*, 82.

38. Philo of Alexandria, *Special Laws* 2.165; Simkovich, *Making of Jewish*

Yet Philo also insists that the Jews must continue to observe Jewish laws, and that the Scriptures' literal meaning must be preserved, not just allegorical meanings that contribute to universalist interpretations. Philo was both a universalist and a particularist. "Israel's special election" could exist side by side with universalism.[39]

The main difference that Simkovich sees between biblical and post-biblical universalism is that the biblical material had universalistic hope for "the far-distant eschatological future," while the later documents envision it happening "in the immediate present."[40]

In this regard, the important apocalyptic work *First Enoch* resembles the Bible, in that it envisions the salvation of righteous Gentiles in the future. *First Enoch* envisions a sort of heavenly Messiah figure, whom it calls the Son of Man or the Chosen One. "That son of man . . . will be the light of the nations, and he will be a hope for those who grieve in their hearts. All who dwell on the earth will fall down and worship before him" (48:2, 4–5).[41] "After this it will be said to the holy ones, that they should seek in heaven the secrets of righteousness, the lot of faith; for the sun has risen upon the earth, and darkness has passed away. There will be light that does not cease . . . The light of truth will endure forever before the Lord of the Spirits" (58:5–6).[42] The "son of man" comes originally from Daniel 7:13, where it stood for the righteous among Israel, to whom "the Ancient of Days" would give "an everlasting dominion" (7:13–14 RSV). In *First Enoch*, the Son of Man is a heavenly savior figure, "a divine figure"[43] with judging and revelatory powers (46:3–4; 49:2–4).

Pseudo-Phocylides is a Jewish document that draws upon Stoic ideas and expresses "Ethical Universalism." Many Jewish details and clues occur in the document, but not "Sabbath, dietary

---

Universalism, 78–79.

39. Simkovich, *Making of Jewish Universalism*, 141.

40. Simkovich, *Making of Jewish Universalism*, 83.

41. *1 Enoch: Hermeneia*, 62.

42. *1 Enoch: Hermeneia*, 72.

43. *1 Enoch: Hermeneia*, 59nc.

law, and circumcision," practices that distinguish Jews from Gentiles. The work presents itself as a product of Greek wisdom, even using the name of a Greek author (Phocylides) mentioned by Plato and Aristotle.[44] Stoic values such as moderation, self-control,[45] and deification[46] are highlighted. The author is harmonizing Jewish and Hellenist values, assuming that "all people may incorporate aspects of Jewish piety into their lives,"[47] yet choosing not to identify them as Jewish.[48]

There was a reciprocal influence between Jewish universalism and Stoicism, much of it taking place in the city of Alexandria.[49] The two sets of literature listed many of the same virtues and vices.[50] Stoic writers also expanded upon Plato's virtue lists.[51] Stoics believed the Logos was present in all human minds, communicating a universal moral law. The Logos is "a part of the mind of God that has descended in to the body."[52] Epictetus said, "You are a principal work, a fragment of God Himself, you have in yourself a part of Him. . . . You bear God about with you, poor wretch, and know it not."[53] The striving for ethical perfection and a feeling of the kinship to all humankind, were primary values within Stoicism.[54] We see this in such celebrated authors as Cicero and Seneca.

Besides sharing a high degree of specificity about the different kinds of interaction with Gentiles that were envisioned, Simkovich

44. Collins, *Jewish Wisdom in the Hellenistic Age*, 159.

45. Simkovich, *Making of Jewish Universalism*, 114.

46. Finlan, "Second Peter's Notion," 41.

47. Simkovich, *Making of Jewish Universalism*, 116.

48. Finlan, "Second Peter's Notion," 42; Collins, *Jewish Wisdom*, 176.

49. Simkovich, *Making of Jewish Universalism*, 122, 125.

50. Simkovich, *Making of Jewish Universalism*, 124. *The Testaments of the Twelve Patriarchs* have some of these virtue and vice lists (135n115). This text, in turn, probably had an influence on the apostle Paul.

51. Simkovich, *Making of Jewish Universalism*, 135, n111.

52. Starr, *Sharers in Divine Nature*, 159, summarizing Seneca, *Epistle* 120.14.

53. Epictetus, *Disc.* 2.8; from *The Stoic and Epicurean Philosophers*, 295.

54. Simkovich, *Making of Jewish Universalism*, 123.

helps us to affirm that there really were strong currents of universalism within Judaism. Some Jewish authors assumed that Greeks and Jews were already worshiping the same God, and that Greeks could learn more about the one God from Jews. Philo and other Jewish writers taught that the universal ethics or universal law that people were seeking was already present in the Jewish law. Other writers freely blend Jewish and Gentile ideas without giving any credit to Jewish sources. There are strong streams of Universalized Worship and Ethical Universalism in Christian teachings.

2

The New Testament Message

What was a new and extraordinary message found in Third Isaiah and in Zechariah is par for the course in the New Testament. The NT message is addressed to everyone, regardless of nationality or identity, and to lose sight of that is to lose the gospel itself. There is no favoritism in the kingdom. No group has any superiority, not Jew or Greek, not rich or poor, not male or female (Gal 3:28; Rom 10:12; Mark 7:24–31). Jesus values the individual experience of each person, yet provides a basis for unifying us in one family. Uniting in one the scattered children of God means that the children have to overcome their provincialism. Although the Jewish evangelists do not want to emphasize it, they cannot help but note that Jesus led the apostles to preach outside of Judaea and Galilee, to Gerasa, Phoenicia, and the Decapolis,[1] primarily Gentile areas. Jesus chose to take them to places where they would have intimate contact with Gentiles. It seems that the four evangelists were all more attached to Jewish particularism than was Jesus himself. The evangelists partially suppress these Gentile-visiting portions of Jesus' mission. But Jesus' own choices show that he wanted to lift people out of the tribalist phase of religious loyalty.

---

1. Mark 5:1; 7:24, 31; Matt 15:21; 8:28 ("the country of the Gadarenes," probably the same as Gerasa); Luke 8:26.

The revelation of Jesus was meant to bring permanent changes to the thinking about salvation.

The gospel demands that we be open to the *other*, the "Samaritan" or the "Ninevite." Jonah despised the Ninevites and did not want to prophesy to them (Jonah 3:10–4:2). Jesus drew attention to the fact that the Ninevites believed Jonah, when the latter finally spoke to them (Matt 12:41; Luke 11:30). Many of Jesus' contemporaries despised the Samaritans as half-breeds and/or as people who had a distorted version of YHWH worship. The Samaritan or the Ninevite in our lives is whoever is vilified or despised—rich or poor, black or white, foreigner or immigrant—anyone we would like to label or reject. Partisan and nationalistic religious loyalty represents backsliding to a primitive and provincialized stage of society. When religion is taken over by political identity, truth and goodness are suffocated. Religious terms and ideas become corrupted to the service of the self and the group, defined in opposition to other groups. When religion is blended with politics, politics takes over and the religious spirit is stifled. The pressure to conform deadens all originality.

THE GOSPEL AS A UNIFYING FORCE

It is the focus on the individual, and God's love for the individual, that distinguishes the New Covenant from the Old. "Unlike Israel whose relationship with God was dominated by holiness enforced by the mediating Temple cult, and where love was configured more to the national identity, the Spirit in the new covenant pours the love of God to deepest level of the *individual's heart*."[2] This attention to the individual, to the one wandering sheep instead of to the ninety-nine, is what stands out. The believing community is not called the new Israel. It is, in fact, an altogether new *kind* of community made up of the *friends* of Jesus, rather than servants (John 15:15). It is a community of Jews, Gentiles, and Samaritans. Some important individual believers were Syro-Phoenician, Gadarene,

---

2. Saucy, "Personal Ethics of the New Covenant," 353.

or Roman. And we know that a group of Greeks came to see Jesus (John 12:20–22).

With Jesus came a new age of spiritual possibilities. The early church realized some of those possibilities. They discovered hope in a way people had never done so before. They set up charitable practices that were unparalleled in the ancient world.[3] Jesus told his followers that people would know they are his disciples by their love for one another (John 13:35). It appears that they fulfilled that promise in the first two centuries.

We can get a taste of those early, miraculous days if we return to the message of God's love, and the astounding new revelation that Jesus brought. We have to be ready for newness. The new truth expands, like new wine does (Mark 2:22). We need to stretch our minds to receive it. Old ways of thinking are like old wineskins that cannot stretch, cannot contain expansive new truth. The Spirit can empower us with the creativity and imagination we need to handle change. Jesus drew attention to the expansiveness of his teachings with the new wine metaphor.

Jesus taught that we are all children of the same Father, and therefore brothers and sisters to each other: "You are all brothers . . . You have one Father, who is in heaven" (Matt 23:8–9 HCSB). It is crucial to understand that Jesus thought of God as the father of each person, not just his own father. Further, there is a link between this relationship to the Father, and the metaphor of all people being brothers and sisters: "Go to my brothers and say to them, 'I am ascending to my Father and your Father, to my God and your God'" (John 20:17).

This must be a permanent doctrine of the religion that bears his name. Admission to Jesus' family had one requirement: willingness to do the will of God (Mark 3:35; John 7:17). Membership was not dependent upon culture, race, or status, but only on "an honest and good heart" (Luke 8:15). Jesus set in motion a great universalizing power, a spiritual spearhead in the wake of which social changes could happen. Unfortunately, many of these social

---

3. Sanders, *Embracing Prodigals*, 29–30, drawing upon Stark, *Triumph of Christianity*.

changes were suppressed when Christianity became the religion of the empire, when it became entangled with the empire's ideology and values. Christian theology and ethics suffered a setback from which they have still not fully recovered, to this day.

Christianity became the empire's religion. It contributed to unity within the empire, but then was subverted by the political self-interest of the empire, especially when it was enforced by the sword. "Unity," then, largely became a political phenomenon. But Jesus has always been present within the religion that bears his name, ready to stimulate new reformations and rebirths whenever there are hearts and minds that are receptive, that can stretch like new wineskins (Mark 2:22).

The gospel truth gets diluted by adaptation to existing social norms, while political self-interest corrupts it entirely. Religion must be social because humanity is social, but Jesus' religion points out the *inwardness* of personality, changing the world by changing the individual.

Jesus' teaching is personalist, in that it recognizes the significance and freedom of each child of God. "Personality . . . is God's image and idea, the bearer of the divine principle in life."[4] Berdyaev draws out the unique meaning of "personality":

> The individual is born in the racial process; he belongs to the world of nature. Personality, however, is a spiritual and ethical category; it is not born of material, it is spiritually created . . . Personality is not nature, but freedom: it is spirit . . . We may say of the individual that he is part of the race and of society, but an indivisible part. We cannot think of personality as a part of any whole. It is other-worldly, spiritual. Personality breaks into the natural and social order with the claim that it is an end in itself . . . The total, the whole, the primacy of the whole over its parts—this applies only to personality.[5]

Mounier gave something close to a definition of personalism; he said that personalism is not a philosophical system, but an "idea:

---

4. Berdyaev, *Destiny*, 134.

5. Berdyaev, *Beginning*, 125; quoted in his *Christian Existentialism*, 75.

. . . the primacy of the human person over material necessities and collective mechanisms."[6] Jesus focused on the reality of personality and of spiritual relationship with God and others. "Jesus was the first who asserted those rights of human personality which are always in danger of being sacrificed to the interests of the group. He insisted that men are accountable to God, and must have room to serve Him freely, and that the community, whatever form it may assume, must not crush the individual soul."[7] His message would transform *persons*, and persons would then have an effect in the world. "His demand is not for obedience to certain moral laws but for a new will . . . the one thing necessary was a right relation to God—a complete harmony of our will with the divine will . . . His concern is always with the inward principles of man's life, not with the framework."[8]

Religious unity must be founded upon an enlightened personalism complemented with recognition of the all-encompassing unity of Deity. Spiritual unity does not mean conformity. It means a balancing of responsibility and freedom. It saves us from both the tyranny of politics and the anarchy of individualism. Spiritual unity means a shared spiritual motivation accompanied by respect for the differing views of others.

For we have one Father above all and in us all, and we are all brothers. There must be one fold, and one shepherd, who will gather together in unity the scattered children of God, until all of us come to the unity of the faith and of the knowledge of the Son of God.[9]

6. Ligneul, *Teilhard and Personalism*, 4; he quotes Mounier without giving the source.

7. Scott, *Ethical Teaching*, 59. We can forgive the use of "men" in this 1924 book.

8. Scott, *Ethical Teaching*, 39–40, 81.

9. Eph 4:6; Matt 23:8; John 10:16; 11:52; Eph 4:13.

PASSAGES IN MARK

Jesus rides into Jerusalem on a donkey (11:1–7), acting out the Peace King prophecy of Zechariah 9:9–10, although Mark does not quote Zechariah, as Matthew and John do. What follows on the next day is one of the most startling affirmations of the universal worship of God. Jesus "began to drive out those who were selling and those who were buying in the temple, and he overturned the tables of the money-changers" (11:15). He then prophesies against the temple's rulers: "Is it not written, 'My house shall be called a house of prayer for all the nations'? But you have made it a den of robbers" (11:17). In his most radical act of rebellion against the priests, Jesus gives, as part of his rationale, the fact that they have failed to make the temple a house of prayer *for all peoples* (quoting Isaiah 56:7). Interestingly, Matthew and Luke, in their versions of this incident, leave out precisely that most radical phrase, "for all peoples," although they keep "house of prayer" and also the "den of robbers" accusation, which comes from Jeremiah 7:11. This is not surprising in the case of Matthew, with his emphasis on Jesus' ministry to the Jews, but it *is* surprising in the case of the often Gentile-focused Luke, who has a number of universalizing statements, many of them drawing upon the prophet Isaiah. Mark has retained what are likely the original words of Jesus, taken from the radical prophet Third Isaiah.

Jesus was not afraid to offend the narrowly nationalistic people. He asked, "How can the scribes say that the Messiah is the son of David? . . . David himself calls him Lord; so how can he be his son?" (Mark 12:35, 37; cf. Matt 22:42–45). In the ancient world, no father would call his son "Lord," because fathers were assumed to be superior to sons. Jesus is using this Middle Eastern custom as a lever to pry his Jewish audience away from the idea of the Messiah as Son of David. His real point is to reject the nationalistic and militaristic concept of the Messiah as Son of David. The bit about a son not being called a lord, is a means to that end. He is showing them that their own beliefs ought to tell them that the Messiah is something greater than a son of David.

He showed considerable openness to Gentiles, by leading his apostles into "the region of Tyre," healing a Syrophoenician girl (Mark 7:24–30), traversing "by way of Sidon" and into the Decapolis (7:31), a mostly Gentile region, and to the Gentile country of the Gerasenes (5:1; Luke 8:26, 37).

By his healings and his preaching, he is showing that the gospel is meant for the whole world. The good news will be "proclaimed to all nations" (13:10), "proclaimed in the whole world" (14:9).

PASSAGES IN MATTHEW

Jesus' followers came not only from Jewish regions, but "his fame spread throughout all Syria . . . great crowds followed him from Galilee, the Decapolis . . . and from beyond the Jordan" (Matt 4:24–25).

In Matthew, Jesus is approached by a Roman centurion who wants healing for his servant. The centurion says that he knows he gives orders and they are followed, and he believes Jesus need merely give the order and his servant will be healed. The Roman is expressing a belief in an orderly universe, and recognizing that Jesus has authority on the spiritual level. Jesus highlights this Gentile's faith, saying, "Truly, I say to you, not even in Israel have I found such faith" (Matt 8:10). And he goes on to say that many will come into the kingdom from east and west, and will sit down with Abraham and Isaac and Jacob, "while the heirs of the kingdom will be thrown into the outer darkness" (8:11–12). This implies that it is Gentiles who will be coming into the kingdom. This becomes explicit later on: "this good news of the kingdom will be proclaimed throughout the world, as a testimony to all the nations" (24:14).

The story of the Syro-Phoenician woman is repeated in Matthew, and Jesus tells her "Woman, great is your faith!" (15:28). Jesus not only responds positively to these Gentiles, but commends their faith.

The gospel changes lives. "The last are first; the lost are found. Those who were excluded now are included; outsiders become insiders. There is powerful resistance inherent in these dramatic reversals."[10]

Matthew is the only one of the Gospels that has Jesus claim "I was sent only to the lost sheep of the house of Israel" (15:24), but this is contradicted by his ministry to various Gentiles and by the fact that he leads his apostles into Gentile territories, to Gadara and to "the district of Tyre and Sidon" (8:28; 15:21). The supposed restriction to Israel fits Matthew's belief that the message was first for the Jews; only at the end are they told, "Go therefore and make disciples of all nations" (28:19). But the facts that Matthew feels obligated to report show Jesus interacting with Gentiles during his ministry.

Jesus deliberately acted out the peace prophecy of Zechariah 9:9 when he rode into Jerusalem on a donkey (Matt 21:1–7), and Zechariah is quoted in 21:5. It should be obvious that Jesus had choices. He did not have to do this. He *chose* to affirm the donkey-riding Peace King who will "cut off the chariot from Ephraim and the warhorse from Jerusalem; and . . . shall command peace to the nations" (Zech 9:10), in place of the idea of a War King ("you shall break them with a rod of iron," Ps 2:9).

The evangelist builds upon a number of universalizing passages from Isaiah. Recounting some healings early in Jesus' ministry, he says, "This was to fulfill what had been spoken through the prophet Isaiah: 'Here is my servant, whom I have chosen, my beloved, with whom my soul is well pleased. I will put my Spirit upon him, and he will proclaim justice to the Gentiles. . . . And in his name the Gentiles will hope'" (Matt 12:17–18, 21; Isa 42:1, 3). Matthew seems to be looking ahead, since the preceding stories involved the healing of Jews in the vicinity of Capernaum, while future healings and promises will involve Gentiles (Matt 15:21–28; 28:19). While Jesus is on the cross, a Roman soldier acknowledges his divine status: "Truly this man was God's Son!" (27:54).

All of humanity will hear the good news: "this good news of the kingdom will be proclaimed throughout the world, as a

---

10. Case-Winters, *God Will Be All*, 134.

testimony to all the nations" (24:14); "Go therefore and make disciples of all nations" (28:19).

PASSAGES IN LUKE AND ACTS

Luke puts a big emphasis on salvation being extended to the Gentiles. The poet Simeon, in the temple, encountering the baby Jesus and his parents, exclaims the saving role that Jesus will play, saying "My eyes have seen your salvation, which you have prepared in the presence of all peoples, a light for revelation to the Gentiles and for glory to your people Israel" (Luke 2:30–32). Isaiah 49:6 is here being applied to Jesus. At the very end of Luke's double work, Paul quotes Isaiah 6:9–10 about "this people" being obstinate, and then proclaims, "Let it be known to you that this salvation of God has been sent to the Gentiles; they will listen" (Acts 28:26, 28).

Jesus offends nationalistic people right at the beginning of his ministry. During his inaugural sermon in Nazareth he announces his mission by identifying it with some Isaiah material ("The Spirit of the Lord is upon me, because he has anointed me to bring good news to the poor. He has sent me to proclaim release to the captives and recovery of sight to the blind, to let the oppressed go free, to proclaim the year of the Lord's favor" (Luke 4:18–19; citing Isaiah 61:1–2; 35:5). The Nazarenes, however, are grumbling about why Jesus doesn't work some wonder there, and Jesus, as a rebuke, tells them that there were many widows in Israel in the time of Elijah, but the prophet was sent to no one but a Gentile widow, and there were many lepers in Israel in the time of the prophet Elisah, but none of them was healed except Naaman, a Syrian (Luke 4:25–27). This offends the Nazarenes, and they grab Jesus and rush him to a cliff to throw him over, but he turns and walks away from them.

Surely his inaugural announcement was a time to try to present his mission in a positive light. He would not have brought up the issue of foreigners unless it were an essential part of his message. Evidently, it *was* essential to his mission to point out that foreigners are included in God's grace, essential enough to risk getting a cold-hearted reception to his message. A few chapters after this initial announcement, we see Jesus preaching to people who came from Tyre and Sidon (Luke 6:17). And then he heals a centurion's servant (7:1–10), and compliments the centurion's faith (7:9). It is the apostle Paul who later organizes these Gentiles into churches, but Jesus had already been preaching and ministering to them.

Also interesting about his quoting of Isaiah 61 during his inaugural speech is the fact that he stops right before the Isaiah text speaks of proclaiming "the day of vengeance of our God" (Isa 61:2). Vengeance is not part of Jesus' mission, and he does not hesitate to leave out a vengeful Scripture. Jesus only uses the part of the Isaiah passage that coincides with his mission.

One of the most interesting passages is where Luke heightens the universalizing potential of a Second Isaiah passage. Isaiah has "In the wilderness prepare the way of the Lord, make straight in the desert a highway for our God . . . Then the glory of the Lord shall be revealed, and all people shall see it together" (40:3, 5). Luke uses this saying to introduce the ministry of John the baptizer, and he heightens the universalism at the end by saying "All flesh shall see the salvation of God" (Luke 3:6). The possible ambiguity of "all people" is made clearer by "all flesh." Jesus is clearly the Messiah for everyone, not just for the Jews.

But Jesus still loves his fellow Jews, as we see when he mourns over Jerusalem's rejection: "How often have I desired to gather your children together as a hen gathers her brood under her wings, and you were not willing!" (Luke 13:34). Still, "forgiveness of sins is to be proclaimed in his name to all nations, beginning from Jerusalem" (24:47). The punch lines of some parables imply Gentiles coming into the kingdom: "people will come from east and west, from north and south, and will eat in the kingdom of God . . . Go into the roads and lanes, and compel people to come in" (13:29; 14:23). Gentiles might even exceed the Jews: "Indeed, some are last who will be first, and some are first who will be last" (13:30). The phrase "all nations" in Luke 24:47 (πάντα τὰ ἔθνη; *panta ta ethnē*) harkens back to the same phrase in Genesis 18:18; 22:18; Isaiah

2:2; 25:6–7,[11] passages about all nations being blessed through Abraham (Gen 22:18) or being delivered from the shroud that is upon all peoples (Isa 25:7).

The Acts of the Apostles begins and ends with a mention of the universal mission: "you will be my witnesses in Jerusalem, in all Judea and Samaria, and to the ends of the earth" (1:8); "this salvation of God has been sent to the Gentiles" (28:28).[12] Paul and Barnabas announce in Pisidian Antioch that "so the Lord has commanded us, saying, 'I have set you to be a light for the Gentiles, so that you may bring salvation to the ends of the earth'" (13:47). Here they appropriate Isaiah 49:6 as their own commission to preach to the Gentiles.[13] And many Gentiles do become believers (13:48).

At the pivotal apostolic council, both Peter and Paul speak up for full inclusion of Gentiles without the requirement of circumcision (15:5, 9, 12). James, the Lord's brother, leader of the Jerusalem church, quotes the prophet Amos to affirm that God "looked favorably on the Gentiles, to take from among them a people for his name . . . so that all other peoples may seek the Lord—even all the Gentiles over whom my name has been called" (Acts 15:14, 17; citing Amos 9:12).[14]

A pattern that recurs in Luke's writings and in Paul's as well, is the idea that the gospel is proclaimed "to the Jew first and also to the Greek" (Rom 1:16; cf. Acts 3:25–26; 18:4–6).

Sometimes the wisdom of the Gentiles is cited in support of the gospel. In his famous speech at the Aeropagus in Athens, Paul sees fit to quote the Greek poet Epimenides, "In him we live and move and have our being," and then he quotes the poet Aratus, "For we too are God's offspring" (Acts 17:28).[15] Greek wisdom contained an anticipation and a hope for a message of salvation such as Jesus brought. Luke and Acts make clear that God's intention is to bring salvation to the ends of the earth.

---

11. Köstenberger and Alexander, *Salvation to the Ends of the Earth*, 119.

12. Köstenberger and Alexander, *Salvation to the Ends of the Earth*, 125.

13. Köstenberger and Alexander, *Salvation to the Ends of the Earth*, 148–49.

14. Köstenberger and Alexander, *Salvation to the Ends of the Earth*, 153.

15. Dupuis, *Toward Religious Pluralism*, 49–50.

PASSAGES IN JOHN

John gives one of the clearest descriptions of the incarnation: the divine Son coming to dwell in human flesh and live a human life. "The Word became flesh and lived among us, and we have seen his glory, the glory as of a father's only son, full of grace and truth" (1:14). As the Word, the preexistent Jesus was creator of this world: "All things came into being through him" (1:3). He came with saving intention, but his spiritual significance often went unrecognized: "the world came into being through him; yet the world did not know him" (1:10). But he saved those who recognized the truth in him: "to all who received him, who believed in his name, he gave power to become children of God" (1:12).

Even one of his enemies unconsciously recognized his saving influence. In debating with his fellow priests, Caiaphas tells them "You do not understand that it is better for you to have one man die for the people than to have the whole nation destroyed" (John 11:50). He was ignorantly speaking more truth than he guessed, thus "he prophesied that Jesus was going to die for the nation, and not for the nation only, but also to unite the scattered children of God" (11:51–52 HCSB). We are not given any explanation about who the scattered children of God are, or what their uniting means. It may be that anyone who believes in the creator God was one of these children of God. Elsewhere in the Gospel, no nationality or background is given, regarding who could be gathered in: "Whoever believes in the Son has eternal life" (3:36). "Whoever comes to me will never be hungry" (6:35).

Therefore, one of the major truths of the gospel is uttered ironically and unknowingly by the high priest. He intends evil, but he utters the truth. Jesus really is gathering all the scattered children of God into a spiritual family.

Truth is characteristic of the gospel of Jesus. The apostle John refers to the spirit that Jesus sent as the Spirit of truth (John 14:17; 15:26; 16:13; 1 John 4:6). Jesus says "When the Spirit of truth comes, he will guide you into all the truth" (16:13). Truth has a magnetic power; it draws those who love the truth: "Everyone who belongs to the truth listens to my voice" (John 18:37). This one is spoken to a Gentile, and it is an open invitation to all.

The spiritual indwelling empowers the love of which he speaks: "If you keep my commandments, you will abide in my love, just as I have kept my Father's commandments and abide in his love" (15:10). Jesus will continue to educate all those who love him: "I do not call you servants any longer . . . but I have called you friends, because I have made known to you everything that I have heard from my Father" (15:15).

In one of his final prayers, Jesus pleads to his Father "that they may be one, as we are one" (John 17:11). They should be able to acquire spiritual unity by the spiritual quality they possess: "The glory that you have given me I have given them, so that they may be one, as we are one" (17:22). An intimate and loving interpenetration of divinity and humanity should lead to unity: "that they may all be one. As you, Father, are in me and I am in you, may they also be in us . . . I in them and you in me, that they may become completely one, so that the world may know that you have sent me and have loved them even as you have loved me" (17:21, 23). Love and unity among believers will verify to the world that God has sent Jesus. And God's love of his Son enlivens his love of human beings: "I made your name known to them, and I will make it known, so that the love with which you have loved me may be in them, and I in them" (17:26). Again, the mutual interpenetration of divinity and humanity is the key to spiritual unity.

In this prayer, Jesus asks the Father, but also broadcasts to his disciples, what he wants. The love they have learned from Jesus should empower the love they will have for each other, a love strong enough to convince the world of Jesus' God-given mission. Believers will have real spiritual power, "glory" (17:22), which assists their unity.

And this message of unity is for all of humanity. The Son has "authority over all people" and he uses it to impart "eternal life to all whom you have given him" (17:2). The Son sends his apostles "into the world . . . so that the world may believe that you have sent me" (17:18, 21). The world currently lies in ignorance, so, "In the world you face persecution. But take courage; I have conquered the world!" (16:33).

Jesus reassures people that they will have a secure home, a place to live and grow in the afterlife, when he says "In my Father's house are many mansions . . . I go to prepare a place for you" (John 14:2–3). The purpose of the afterlife is abundant living and learning and loving—the same as the purpose of *this* life.

A belief held in common by all the evangelists is that "the Kingdom of God has in a real sense become present fact, here and now"; someone greater than Solomon and greater than the temple is here (Luke 11:31; Matt 12:6); "The Kingdom of God, then, is a power already released in the world."[16] "In Jesus Christ, the Son of Man, the Kingdom of God is irrevocably taking possession of the world."[17] In spirit and in potential, Christ has conquered the world. But it needs to become real in time and on the material level, through our lives. "Go and do likewise" (Luke 10:37). Love among believers will testify to everyone: "Just as I have loved you, you also should love one another. By this everyone will know that you are my disciples" (13:34–35).

PAUL'S LETTERS

Especially in Paul's letters do we see an impulse to extend the good news to the whole world. Paul says that God "was pleased to reveal his Son to me, so that I might proclaim him among the Gentiles" (Gal 1:15–16).

For Paul, Jesus inaugurated a new age, but the fullness of this new age will not be seen until his glorious return. Jesus "defeated the powers of sin, death, and the flesh"; yet, all those still exist until "the kingdom of God [is] manifested in its fullness. Thus Christians live in a time between the times: between the times of Christ's resurrection and their own . . . between the times of

---

16. Bright, *Kingdom of God*, 216, 218.
17. Rahner, "Jesus Christ. IV," 769.

the kingdom's beginnings and its completeness."[18] It is the future change that he is referring to when he writes "At the name of Jesus every knee should bend, in heaven and on earth and under the earth, and every tongue should confess that Jesus Christ is Lord" (Phil 2:10–11). He has "power . . . to make all things subject to himself" (Phil 3:21). If all people become subject to Jesus, if all worship God, and if all are made alive in Christ, then all will be spiritually united (made harmonious, allied, loving) as well. The whole world is the target of God's intentions: "In Christ God was reconciling the world to himself" (2 Cor 5:19).

Believers will be transformed, degree by degree, into Jesus' image: "all of us, with unveiled faces, seeing the glory of the Lord as though reflected in a mirror, are being transformed into the same image from one degree of glory to another" (2 Cor 3:18). It is quite logical for there to be stages in our spiritual growth, just as there are stages of growth in our *earth* life. This fits in with Jesus' own teaching about stages of growth: "first the stalk, then the head, then the full grain in the head" (Mark 4:28). Paul emphasizes the new age that Jesus brought. Jesus came "to set us free from the present evil age" (Gal 1:4). And now, "if anyone is in Christ, there is a new creation . . . everything has become new!" (2 Cor 5:17). Salvation means accepting new life, a new attitude, even a new *altitude* of living.

God will perfect all the believers, transform and renew their minds, reveal his will to them (Rom 12:2), and make sure that "individually we are members one of another" (Rom 12:5). "Love is the fulfilling of the law" (13:10). Believers will be filled "with all joy and peace in believing" (15:13). Spiritual transformation is coming for all who believe.

Christ will bring the whole cosmos into order: "Then comes the end, when he hands over the kingdom to God the Father, when he has brought to an end all rule and all authority and power" (1 Cor 15:24 NET). Christ is asserting his power over the celestial powers, in order to allow God's power to permeate everything: "When all things are subjected to him, then the Son himself will

18. Clapp, *Naming Neoliberalism*, 70.

also be subjected to the one who put all things in subjection under him, so that God may be all in all" (1 Cor 15:28). For all believers, he prays that "Christ is formed in you" (Gal 4:19). Christ is perfecting the individual believer, the Christian congregation, and the whole cosmos.

Christians are to "bear one another's burdens" (Gal 6:2) and to "outdo one another in showing honor" (Rom 12:10). Unselfish devotion shall characterize the believing community. Believers are to bear the "fruit of the spirit . . . love, joy, peace, patience, kindness, generosity, faithfulness, gentleness, and self-control" (Gal 5:22–23). In fact, "the whole law is summed up in a single commandment, 'You shall love your neighbor as yourself'" (Gal 5:14). Here, Paul affirms the inner and spiritual meaning of the law, and the spiritual meaning becomes the real meaning.

Paul's love teaching builds upon Jesus' teaching. When Jesus gives the dual love commandment, to love God with all your heart and soul and to love your neighbor as yourself (Matt 22:37–39), he finishes by saying "On these two commandments hang all the law and the prophets" (22:40). The foundation of the law turns out to be love. Paul repeats this principle.

Paul's vision for Jewish and Gentile unity was "two peoples coming together to become one assembly of God's people, to shape a new form of life from these two cultures under the lordship of Jesus Christ and in the power of the Holy Spirit."[19] Paul did not envision the obliteration of the distinction between Jew and Gentile or the homogenization of all human groups. He *did* envision an end to class, ethnic, and gender hierarchies in the kingdom: "There is no longer Jew or Greek, there is no longer slave or free, there is no longer male and female; for all of you are one in Christ Jesus" (Gal 3:28).

Identity in Paul's communities will be shaped by faith, hope, and love (1 Cor 13:13). He makes faith-loyalty, and not ethnicity, class, or gender identity the defining element in membership in the faith-community. Christ died "to set us free from the present evil age" (Gal 1:4), and he also "loved me and gave himself for

19. Harink, *Paul among the Postliberals*, 221.

me" (Gal 2:20). Christ is alive "in you [plural]" (Rom 8:10–11), and also "to me, living is Christ" (Phil 1:21). "Individually we are members one of another," and "all of you are one in Christ Jesus" (Rom 12:5; Gal 3:28). Paul's interests are indeed ecclesial, but his message of universal invitation and spiritual freedom opens up new possibilities for the individual. "For freedom Christ has set us free" (Gal 5:1). In fact, a reining in of this newly released power of the individual will be a major endeavor of some churchmen for the next several centuries (most vividly seen in the Pastoral Epistles [see "Later Epistles," below] and in Ignatius of Antioch).

Universalists are particularly fond of Paul. I am not making an argument for universalism of the type that believes that *all* persons will, eventually, be saved, but there are plenty of biblical passages that *can* be understood in that way, and that also entail harmony among human beings on this earth, even if their main emphasis is on salvation in the long run. "As all die in Adam, so all will be made alive in Christ" (1 Cor 15:22). "By the one man's obedience the many will be made righteous" (Rom 5:19). Paul, of course, is the apostle to the Gentiles. He insists that God always intended to call the Gentiles. "As indeed he says in Hosea, 'Those who were not my people I will call "my people" . . . And in the very place where it was said to them, "You are not my people," there they shall be called children of the living God'" (Rom 9:25–26). Many times he draws upon Scriptures to say that the Gentiles will praise the Lord. He says that his whole mission was "in order that the Gentiles might glorify God for his mercy. As it is written, 'Therefore I will confess you among the Gentiles, and sing praises to your name'" (Rom 15:9, quoting 2 Sam 22:50; Ps 18:49) In the next verse he quotes Deuteronomy 32:43, and in v. 11 he quotes Psalm 117:1; he culminates the passage with: "and again Isaiah says, 'The root of Jesse shall come, the one who rises to rule the Gentiles; in him the Gentiles shall hope'" (Rom 15:12; Isa 11:10).

The Corinthian correspondence is bristling with allusions to, and quotations of, Isaiah. Towards the end of the first letter, Paul says an unbeliever "will bow down before God and worship him, declaring, 'God is really among you'" (1 Cor 14:25). The "you" are the Jews. The language of "bowing down" and "God is among you" comes from Isaiah 45:14. There are several allusions and single-word connections to material in Isaiah 43–49 in 2 Corinthians 5:16–6:2. Old things passed away, and everything is new (2 Cor 5:17; drawing on Isa 42:9; 43:18–19; 48:6). Not charging trespasses (5:19) refers to the blotting out of transgressions in Isaiah 43:25.[20] First Corinthians has a universalizing statement regarding the way that the Spirit gives different gifts to different people: "Now there are varieties of gifts, but the same Spirit; and there are varieties of services, but the same Lord" (1 Cor 12:4–5).

The kind of universalism that I see in Paul is well-described by Daniel Boyarin, who is worth quoting at length:

> Paul was motivated by a Hellenistic desire for the One, which among other things produced an ideal of a universal human essence, beyond difference and hierarchy. This universal humanity, however, was predicated (and still is) on the dualism of the flesh and the spirit, such that while the body is particular, marked through practice as Jew or Greek, and through anatomy as male or female, the spirit is universal . . . Just as the human being is divided into a fleshy and a spiritual component, so is language itself. It is composed of outer, material signs and inner, spiritual significations.[21]

One example of this inner-outer, spiritual-literal distinction is this: "a person is not a Jew who is one outwardly, nor is true circumcision something external and physical. A person is a Jew who is one inwardly, and real circumcision is a matter of the heart—it is spiritual and not literal" (Rom 2:28–29). It is the inner, spiritual dedication and sincerity that really matter. A Gentile can have this dedication as surely as can a Jew. "In one stroke, by interpreting circumcision as referring to a spiritual and not corporeal reality, Paul made it possible for Judaism to become a world religion."[22]

---

20. Wilk, "Isaiah in 1 and 2 Corinthians," 150–51.
21. Boyarin, *Radical Jew*, 7.
22. Boyarin, *Radical Jew*, 230.

The particular *kind* of Judaism to which Boyarin is referring is what we now call Christianity.

The claims of the Torah are limited. Christ believers are not "under the law," subject to the obligations of Torah (1 Cor 9:20; Gal 3:23–25; 5:1–6), yet the Torah's inner meaning was to testify to the Messiah or (more often) to the church.[23] Thus, "the letter of the Law is abrogated; its spirit is fulfilled."[24] The law had a temporary role, comparable to that of a chaperone.[25] "The law was our disciplinarian until Christ came, so that we might be justified by faith. But now that faith has come, we are no longer subject to a disciplinarian, for in Christ Jesus you are all children of God through faith" (Gal 3:24–26). "Children" are accorded respect that is not given to slaves (Gal 4:7); children can outgrow the need for a disciplinarian.

The law had a prophetic function. Typological interpretation, in which a *typos*—a character or an image—in Scripture carries special spiritual meaning, fulfilled in another image in a later text or a later life, has an inherently prophetic implication. Paul uses typology when he says that the waters of the sea through which the Israelites passed were a prefiguration of the waters of baptism. They "were baptized into Moses . . . and all drank the same spiritual drink. For they drank from the spiritual rock that followed them, and the rock was Christ . . . These things occurred as examples [*typoi*] for us" (1 Cor 10:2–4, 6). Not only did the passing through the waters prefigure baptism, but the rock that followed them in the wilderness actually *was* Christ. God intended all along to extend salvation to the Gentiles (Rom 15:9–12).

The allegory of the veil and the shining that appears in 2 Corinthians 3 further illustrates the literal-spiritual dichotomy. Paul contrasts the dead "letter" with the living Spirit: "the letter brings death, but the Spirit gives life" (2 Cor 3:6). "The ministry of death [was] chiselled in letters on stone tablets," but "the ministry of the Spirit [has] come in glory" (2 Cor 3:7–8). However, even the old

---

23. Hays, *Echoes of Scripture*, xiii, 99–108, 121.

24. Boyarin, *Radical Jew*, 7.

25. Dunn, *Theology of Paul*, 143–44.

ministry came with a certain glory. Moses had to put on a veil to shield the Israelites from the spiritual shining of his face (Exod 34:30–33), but that glory is outshone now by "the greater glory" (2 Cor 3:10). Moses' veil becomes a useful symbol for Paul, standing for the self-blindedness of those who read the Law in a literal or material way. "Indeed, to this very day whenever Moses is read, a veil lies over their minds; but when one turns to the Lord, the veil is removed" (3:15–16). The literal-minded reading of the Scriptures is like a veil "which prevents them from perceiving the glory of the truth."[26] The veil may also stand for a kind of restriction on freedom, for "where the Spirit of the Lord is, there is freedom" (3:17). The greater glory leads to freedom and to transformation "from one degree of glory to another" (3:17–18).

All of this does not mean that the Jewish people are rejected or replaced. Paul makes it clear that the Jewish people may be "a disobedient and contrary people" (Rom 10:21), but God has not rejected them (11:1). Jewish intransigence is temporary, and "through their stumbling salvation has come to the Gentiles" (Rom 11:11). God will save the Jews in the end. Jews who, through their unbelief in the Messiah, allowed themselves to be cut off of God's olive tree, will be grafted back in: "how much more will these natural branches be grafted back into their own olive tree" (11:24). After "the full number of the Gentiles has come in," then "all Israel will be saved" (11:25–26). When any, Jew or Gentile, come to believe in the Messiah, they become citizens of heaven (Phil 3:20), and "everything has become new!" (2 Cor 5:17).

This is enabled by the Spirit, and the Spirit is "a first installment" of the blessings that God will give (2 Cor 1:22). The Spirit is a taste "of God's future for creation."[27] "Live by the Spirit," Paul says, "and do not gratify the desires of the flesh" (Gal 5:16). Paul is an ascetic, and sees a sharp conflict between Spirit and flesh. "For what the flesh desires is opposed to the Spirit, and what the Spirit desires is opposed to the flesh . . . Now the works of the flesh are obvious: fornication, impurity, licentiousness, idolatry,

26. Boyarin, *Radical Jew*, 101.
27. Edwards, *Breath of Life*, 111.

sorcery, enmities, strife," and more (5:17, 19–20). Paul issues many harsh warnings about the strivings of the flesh. "To set the mind on the flesh is death, but to set the mind on the Spirit is life and peace" (Rom 8:6). This sharp conflict stands near the beginning of Christianity, and has had a huge influence on Christian morality and psychology ever since. As Peter Brown wrote, "In the future, a sense of the presence of 'Satan,' in the form of a constant and ill-defined risk of lust, lay like a heavy shadow in the corner of every Christian church."[28]

What Paul taught was a universalism "born of the union of Hebraic monotheism and Greek desire for unity and univocity."[29] This has a downside to it, Boyarin says, since it means Paul is advocating not only equality but a kind of "sameness," and suppressing "difference . . . dissolving all others into a single essence in which matters of cultural practice are irrelevant and only faith in Christ is significant."[30] This may be an inevitable by-product of universalism, at least to some degree and when certain contrasts are made.

However, Paul was not able to envision the elimination of all distinctions being thoroughly applied on the fleshly level. The radicalism of the Galatians 3:28 vision was a bit too much to find full social realization. "Paul called for freedom" but he "settled for something else, something less than his vision called for, and thus the continuation of the domestic slavery of marriage for those not called to the celibate life . . . An eradication of male and female and the corresponding social hierarchy is possible only on the level of the spirit, either in ecstasy at baptism or perhaps permanently for the celibate."[31]

Paul concludes that many would not be able to function at a high spiritual level. He allows that many need to function on the fleshly level. For those, marriage is an acceptable option, better than promiscuity but not as good as celibacy: "To the unmarried and the widows I say that it is well for them to remain unmarried

28. Brown, *Body and Society*, 55.
29. Boyarin, *Radical Jew*, 106.
30. Boyarin, *Radical Jew*, 9.
31. Boyarin, *Radical Jew*, 193.

as I am. But if they are not practicing self-control, they should marry. For it is better to marry than to be aflame with passion . . . He who marries his fiancée does well; and he who refrains from marriage will do better" (1 Cor 7:8–9, 38).

Despite the limitations Paul placed upon his own vision, his vision has had a strong influence upon subsequent Christian reflection. The prominence of spiritual unity and individual spiritual growth in Christian theology owe much to Paul's teaching. I would like to discover what could happen with Paul's universalistic ideas if the anti-sexual bias were removed, if the glorification of celibacy were dropped, and if the radicalism of Galatians 3:28 were truly practiced. What progress could be made if gender, class, and ethnic hierarchies were truly overcome? And if what was needed among people was full respect, and not sameness? This would enable the spiritual ideals of Jesus and Paul to manifest in a profound and world-changing way. If people the world over made their supreme goal the determination to do the will of God (Mark 3:35; John 7:17), they would realize a level of truth and fellowship never before known. And if we could respect the motivation of others who have made the same determination, then we would experience spiritual unity. Then "all flesh shall see the salvation of God" (Luke 3:6).

There is a place for "differences" in this scenario, as long as people adopt the attitude that Einstein expressed: "To be a Jew means to bear a serious responsibility not only to his own community, but also toward humanity."[32] Identity differences do not need to mean hostilities.

EPHESIANS

I agree with scholars who consider Ephesians to be written by a disciple of Paul, building on Paul's ideas, but expressing some ideas about the church that are never expressed by Paul in the

---

32. Einstein, *Out of My Later Years*, 262.

"undisputed letters."[33] But when it comes to unity, Ephesians seems pretty close to Paul's own thinking. Ephesians 4 is the most unity-intensive chapter in the Bible. The author exhorts the reader to "maintain the unity of the Spirit in the bond of peace" (4:3). This indicates that the unity is already there; it needs to be *maintained*, rather than created.[34] The bases of unity follow: "There is one body and one Spirit, just as you were called to the one hope of your calling, one Lord, one faith, one baptism, one God and Father of all, who is above all and through all and in all" (4:4–6). The body is the community of believers; they are endowed with one Spirit and they share the same hope. They have one Lord (Jesus), one faith (belief), one baptism (representing spiritual rebirth), and there is one God the Father. Jesus gave us a diversity of spiritual gifts and talents, all for the purpose of "building up the body of Christ, until all of us come to the unity of the faith and of the knowledge of the Son of God, to maturity, to the measure of the full stature of Christ" (4:12–13). A direct linkage is made between social unity and personal character growth. Spiritual gifts are for spiritual edification, and will lead to the final "unity of the faith," presumably something more complete than the initial unity that already existed. The author emphasizes maturity, which shields one from being "tossed to and fro and blown about by every wind of doctrine" (4:14). Evidently there are already theological arguments in the community, which we also see evidenced in the letters of Paul and John. The author uses the metaphor of the body, with Christ as the head; the body is knit together and works properly, "building itself up in love" (4:15–16). Love is both community building and personal growing.

Healthy living in the community requires a rejection of fleshly living and an experience of spiritual transformation. "Be renewed in the spirit of your minds . . . clothe yourselves with the new self" (4:23–24). Truth is to be our guide; we must repudiate anger, lying,

33. The undisputed letters are 1 Thessalonians, Galatians, 1 and 2 Corinthians, Romans, Philemon, and Philippians. Dunn, *Theology of Paul*, 13.

34. One of the main points of Lloyd-Jones, *Basis of Christian Unity*, for instance 22–24, 40–41.

thieving, and we must "not grieve" the Holy Spirit (4:30). Finally, we are to be "forgiving one another, as God in Christ has forgiven you" (4:31).

Unity is inseparable from transformed living and ethical relating. We are to be imitators of God and Christ (5:1–2). Fornication and debauchery are to be rejected (5:3, 18). Husbands and wives are to be loving and respectful: "Each of you, however, should love his wife as himself, and a wife should respect her husband" (5:33), with a little more exhortation being directed to the wives. Wives are to "be subject to your husbands . . . For the husband is the head of the wife" (5:22–23), while "husbands should love their wives" (5:28). "Husbands, love your wives, just as Christ loved the church and gave himself up for her" (5:25). The strong emphasis on mutuality is a challenge to prevailing Greco-Roman beliefs, but this is not the modern idea of full political equality. The wife is told to be subject to the husband (5:22, 24), but the husband is never told to be subject to the wife. All we can say is that Ephesians takes a big step toward the idea of equality, but does not fully reach it.

Ephesians expresses an idea of God bringing about perfection through and *in* Christ. God's will is "set forth in Christ, as a plan for the fullness of time, to gather up all things in him, things in heaven and things on earth . . . far above all rule and authority and power and dominion" (1:9–10, 21). Jesus is gathering all things on earth and above the earth under his control. These rulers, authorities, and powers are celestial figures who turned to evil.[35] God "has put all things under his feet and has made him the head over all things for the church" (1:22).

Jesus has eliminated the barrier between Jews and Gentiles. God has broken down the enmity that was between Jews and Gentiles: "He has abolished the law with its commandments and ordinances, so that he might create in himself one new humanity in place of the two, thus making peace" (2:15). Through Jesus, "both of us have access in one Spirit to the Father" (2:18). Jesus is the real glue that holds the community together: "with Christ Jesus

---

35. Eph 3:10; 6:12; Arnold, *Colossian Syncretism*, 182–84; Dunn, *Theology of Paul*, 106–9.

himself as the cornerstone. In him the whole structure is joined together and grows into a holy temple in the Lord" (2:20–21). And so, "Gentiles have become fellow-heirs, members of the same body, and sharers in the promise in Christ Jesus through the gospel. . . . so that through the church the wisdom of God in its rich variety might now be made known to the rulers and authorities in the heavenly places" (3:6, 10). Part of Christ's mission is to put the rulers and authorities in their place. The believer struggles "against the rulers, against the authorities, against the cosmic powers of this present darkness, against the spiritual forces of evil in the heavenly places" (6:12). The believer must struggle for God and "against the wiles of the devil" (6:11). This echoes Paul's intense struggle between spirit and flesh (Rom 6:13; 8:5–14). Neither Paul nor the author of Ephesians seems to be aware of the sayings of Jesus that indicate the devil has been defeated: "Now is the judgment of this world; now the ruler of this world will be driven out" (John 12:31); "I watched Satan fall from heaven" (Luke 10:18).

The "fullness" (πλήρωμα *plērōma*) is an important concept in Ephesians. It can be connected with the church or with Christ or Christ's influence: "his body, the fullness of him who fills all in all" (1:23); "know the love of Christ that surpasses knowledge, so that you may be filled with all the fullness of God" (3:19). This is related to the idea that Christ, between his first advent and his second advent, is perfecting and gathering together the whole cosmos; God will "gather up all things in him, things in heaven and things on earth" (1:10). Jesus is in charge of the final perfecting and organizing of the cosmos.

LATER EPISTLES

Paul's universalizing tendencies are continued by his successors in the Pastoral Epistles. "God our Savior . . . desires everyone to be saved and to come to the knowledge of the truth" (1 Tim 2:3–4). "The grace of God has appeared, bringing salvation to all" (Titus

2:11).[36] The churches envisioned in the Pastoral Epistles appear to be largely Gentile in makeup. They have an organized hierarchy of overseers, deacons, and elders that suggests a later phase of development than can be seen in Paul's lifetime.[37] It is stated that God "desires everyone to be saved" (1 Tim 2:4). God "is the Savior of all people, especially of those who believe" (1 Tim 4:10). But the Pastorals are only partially helpful to the cause of spiritual unity, since they spend so much time scolding various groups: "younger widows" (1 Tim 5:11), "older women" (Titus 2:3; 1 Tim 4:7), "older men" (Titus 2:2), "teachers" who lead astray (2 Tim 4:3; 1 Tim 4:1). Issues of authority and especially of image and reputation (Titus 2:7–8) have become dominant by the time the Pastorals are written. The Pastoral author is concerned that Christians not appear controversial or nonconformist. A church overseer "must be above reproach . . . respectable . . . well thought of by outsiders, so that he may not fall into disgrace" (1 Tim 3:2, 7).

The author of 1 Timothy is particularly nervous about "younger widows" because of their "sensual desires" (1 Tim 5:11), and their love of "gadding about from house to house" (5:13). Rather, let them "marry, bear children, and manage their households" (5:14), but never presume to "teach or to have authority over a man; she is to keep silent" (2:12), for "she will be saved through childbearing" (2:15). This cannot be harmonized with the historical Paul, who only tolerated marriage as second best, and who recognized women as leaders in the churches (Phil 4:2–3; 1 Cor 1:11), even to the point of naming a woman apostle, Junia (Rom 16:7). The Pastorals reflect the views of the winning party in the battle over Paul's legacy. In the Pastorals, "Paul" is domesticated and made to conform to prevailing Greco-Roman social views. The radical Paul of 1 Corinthians 1:27–31 and Galatians 3:26–28 is replaced with the stern hierarch who says "Let a woman learn in silence with full submission" (1 Tim 2:11).

36. See Ramelli, *Larger Hope?*, 18.

37. Finlan, *Apostle Paul*, 166, 170; MacDonald, *Pauline Churches*, 44, 203–4, 207.

The hope for universal salvation is also found in Second Peter: "The Lord . . . is patient with you, not wanting any to perish, but all to come to repentance" (2 Pet 3:9). But this author is also concerned about "false prophets" with their "destructive opinions" and "scoffers . . . indulging their own lusts" (2:1; 3:3). Social battles about authority, morality, gender, and public perception were rife in the church in the late first and early second centuries.

REVELATION

Revelation is not particularly amenable, at first glance, to the idea of the spiritual unification of humanity. It is much more dualistic than that, with "saints" on one side and "idolaters" on the other, with a grim fate in store for the latter (e.g., Rev 21:8; 22:15). But there is a vision of the cleansing and renovation of the universe at the end, even "a new heaven and a new earth . . . and . . . the new Jerusalem . . . prepared as a bride," with a promise that "the home of God is among mortals. He will dwell with them; they will be his peoples, and God himself will be with them; he will wipe away every tear from their eyes. Death will be no more" (21:1–4). These are peoples of all nationalities. "They will be my children" (21:7). By giving up his life, Christ "ransomed for God saints from every tribe and language and people" (5:9).

The Seer gazes upon "a great multitude that no one could count, from every nation, from all tribes and peoples and languages standing before the throne and before the Lamb, robed in white" (7:9). Picking up on images from Isaiah and Ezekiel, the Seer writes, "And the city has no need of sun or moon to shine on it, for the glory of God is its light . . . The nations will walk by its light, and the kings of the earth will bring their glory into it" (21:23–24). "People will bring into it the glory and the honor of the nations" (21:26). The new heavens and new earth draws upon Isaiah 65:17; 66:22. The new Jerusalem coming down from heaven, adorned as a bride (21:2), draws upon Isaiah 62:5. The wiping away of all tears and the absence of death come from Isaiah

25:8; 65:20.[38] The nations bringing their wealth and kings coming to minister draw upon Isaiah 60:6, 10–11. There is "an *end-time conversion* of the nations."[39]

It truly is an international vision. The "eternal gospel" is proclaimed "to every nation and tribe and language and people" (14:6). In the new Jerusalem, there is a tree of life, "and the leaves of the tree are for the healing of the nations" (22:2). This blissful future is not for everyone, indiscriminately given, but only for "those who conquer," those who do not practice "abomination or falsehood, but only those who are written in the Lamb's book of life" (21:7, 27). This vision of spiritual uniting is only for those who are truthful and loyal to the Messiah. "See, I am coming soon; my reward is with me, to repay according to everyone's work. I am the Alpha and the Omega" (22:12–13).

Not all of the New Testament follows Revelation's scenario of apocalyptic judgment of the world, but the idea that the return of Jesus will bring the repair and restoration of the human race is present throughout the New Testament. With Paul, the first coming of Jesus inaugurated a new age, but the full implications of this new age will not be manifested until Jesus' return. This is what Luke also envisions: the "universal restoration that God announced long ago through his holy prophets" (Acts 3:21).

38. Mathewson, "Isaiah in Revelation," 201–3.
39. Mathewson, "Isaiah in Revelation," 207.

3

Christian Teachings on Unity
The Imperative to Unity

We have seen that the teaching on spiritual unity comes from Jesus himself: "I in them and you in me, that they become completely one, so that the world may know that you have sent me and have loved them even as you have loved me" (John 17:23). "There will be one flock, one shepherd" (John 10:16). "Love your neighbor as yourself" (Matt 22:39). "My house shall be called a house of prayer for all the nations" (Mark 11:17).

Christianity has faltered on this ideal more than on any other aspect of Jesus' teaching, having failed to see that spiritual unity is truly a *spiritual* product, and not an institutional or doctrinal one. Christians have tended to focus on creeds and church structures, which is not where spiritual unity will be found. Real spiritual unity is in the realm of experience and mutual respect, of lives lived in harmony with the Spirit and with generosity and understanding toward others. It does not mean mental uniformity, but spiritual synchrony, mutual respect, and understanding between those who may think of God differently. The secret of spiritual unity is the dedication of different people to the will of God: "Whoever does the will of my Father in heaven is my brother and sister and mother" (Matt 12:50).

Unfortunately, with the Emperor Constantine (early fourth century AD) and especially the Emperor Theodosius (late fourth century), the church and state started working together to impose unity by force. "The two visible realities, church and world, were fused."[1] Christianity became an imperial religion, corrupted by the state's power. "State, economy, art, rhetoric, superstition, and war have all been baptized."[2] This continues whenever churches make alliances with governments. "The Constantinian heresy ultimately reverts to a purely pagan view of God as a tribal deity."[3]

There has been a constant conflict ever since between the Jesus method of persuasion and love and the imperial method of coercion and conformity. This also replays the conflict between the concepts of a nurturing God and an authoritarian God.

> The attempt to reverse the New Testament relationship of church and world, making faith invisible and the Christianization of the world a historic achievement with the institutional forms, was undertaken in good faith but has backfired, having had the sole effect of raising the autonomy of unbelief to a higher power . . . The short-circuited means used to 'Christianize' 'responsibly' the world in some easier way than by the gospel have had the effect of dechristianizing the Occident.[4]

There really is evil in the world, and the attempt to superficially Christianize the world only makes Christianity itself superficial.

Before the imperial corruption took place, the early church had emphasized profound spiritual transformation.

DEIFICATION OF BELIEVERS

Part of the process of the perfecting of the kingdom is the matter of the perfecting of individual believers. It is present in Jesus'

1. Yoder, "Otherness of the Church," 57.
2. Yoder, "Otherness of the Church," 57.
3. Yoder, "Peace without Eschatology?," 157.
4. Yoder, "Peace without Eschatology?," 61.

teaching: "Be perfect, therefore, as your heavenly Father is perfect" (Matt 5:48). Of course, fulfilling this mandate requires time: a lifetime here, and a long period of time in the heavenly kingdom. It is a process of progressive divinizing and spiritual transformation. Paul says it best: "Where the Spirit of the Lord is, there is freedom. And all of us . . . are being transformed into the same image from one degree of glory to another" (2 Cor 3:17–18). Transformation proceeds through stages, in this life and the next. It turns out that salvation is also transformation, and transformation is also deification. All of it happens by degrees and in stages, which suggests a plan.

John talks about deification when he says "we are God's children now; what we will be has not yet been revealed. What we do know is this: when he is revealed, we will be like him" (1 John 3:2). To become like Jesus is certainly deification. If you are like Jesus, then you have astounding spiritual character, faith, and loyalty. Paul says we are "to be conformed to the image of his Son" (Rom 8:29). Christians are meant not only to learn from the life of the divine Son, but to make spiritual progress toward Jesus' own nature. We are to be spiritual kin to Jesus himself, and he himself indicated this was possible: "Whoever does the will of God is my brother and sister and mother" (Mark 3:35). Being children in God's family entails ethical treatment of all the other children in the family. "You are all brethren . . . for you have one Father, who is in heaven" (Matt 23:8–9 RSV).

Deification means real spiritual progress, the taking on (to a limited degree) of the qualities of God. It is real and permanent spiritual change. Becoming like Jesus is the goal and ideal of every Christian. We are God's children now, and we are increasingly being spiritually transformed into Christ's likeness. Second Peter says, "You . . . may become partakers of the divine nature" (2 Pet 1:4 RSV). What an astounding promise! It is a mandate for unending spiritual progress toward the goal of perfection, a mandate that will be most fully realized in the afterlife, but which becomes part of our experience in this lifetime. It has profound ethical implications.

Closely connected with the teachings of deification is the biblical teaching that Jesus was either the creator or co-creator of this world. "All things came into being through him, and without him not one thing came into being" (John 1:3). Paul says "for us there is one God, the Father, from whom are all things and for whom we exist, and one Lord, Jesus Christ, through whom are all things and through whom we exist" (1 Cor 8:6). Similarly, in Hebrews God created the worlds (plural) through Jesus: "through whom he also created the worlds" (Heb 1:2). These passages speak of creation "through" Jesus, using the same preposition: (διά [*dia*]). Colossians makes the same point with a different preposition: "He is the image of the invisible God . . . in (ἐν [*en*]) him all things in heaven and on earth were created" (Col 1:15–16).

Jesus is the creative power who created the stars, the planets, and life itself. This creative power is really the same power by which he healed people, and then by which he raised himself from the dead: "I have power to lay it down, and I have power to take it up again" (John 10:18). First his power created life itself. During his ministry, his reputation as having power drew people to him to be healed (Luke 6:19). Then he used his teaching power to try to reach their minds and their hearts, and to contribute to their spiritual growth. At the end, he used his power to raise himself up. And finally, his power and God's power will raise *us* up, after our deaths: "we will live with him by the power of God" (2 Cor 13:4). This power will someday transform the human race.

Creator Christology is a central principle of the biblical teaching about salvation, deification, and the transformation of humanity. Creator Christology will also play a key role in my later discussion of theological pluralism and spiritual unity.

PATRISTIC TEACHING

A number of early Christians believed that when Jesus returned he would set up an earthly kingdom centered in Jerusalem. Such millennialist thought imagined a perfected human society. "Justin writes . . . of the idyllic millennium, when Jerusalem will be rebuilt and enlarged and Christians, along with the patriarchs and prophets, will dwell there with Christ in perfect felicity."[5] However, millennialist thought eventually became a minor stream within Christian belief.

Much more promising is the stream known as universalism. Here, "universalism" refers to the widespread Christian belief that all souls will eventually be saved. Universalism has significant overlaps with the theme of the spiritual uniting of humanity, and therefore I draw upon it, not to affirm universalism as defined here, but to affirm some of the faith assertions made in connection with it.

The main concern of early Christians was the salvation of souls, not the rectification of earthly society, and they had much to say about the saving and spiritual perfecting of souls, but remarkably little to say about how this might affect civil society on earth. Still, there are deposits of spiritual wealth in Christian universalism to be mined in search of reflection upon the perfecting of the human race.

For instance, Bardaisan was a Syriac Christian with an intellectualizing bent, who wrote "once that new world will be constituted, all evil movements will cease, all rebellions will come to an end, and the fools will be persuaded, and the lacks will be filled, and there will be safety and peace, as a gift of the Lord of all natures."[6] This envisions humanity deeply and permanently changed.

A more well-known theologian was Clement of Alexandria, who taught, "'The God of the universe has disposed everything for universal salvation . . .' Repentance is therefore not limited to our earthly life, but can take place 'both here on earth and elsewhere, because tis no place where God does not do good.'"[7] Even in hell, God can save: "The Lord brought the good news even to those who were in hell . . . God's punishments save and educate!"[8]

---

5. Kelly, *Early Christian Doctrines*, 466.

6. *Book of the Laws of Countries*; translation by Ramelli, *Larger Hope?*, 22.

7. *Stromata* (*Books of Miscellany*) 7:2:12 and 4:6:37:7; translation by Ramelli, *Larger Hope?*, 26.

8. *Strom.* 6:6:45–47; translation by Ramelli, *A Larger Hope?*, 26.

Clement thought that God prepared the Greeks, just as he prepared the Hebrews, for the divine advent. "To the ones he [the Lord] gave the commandments, to the others philosophy . . . Philosophy, therefore, was a preparation, paving the way for him who is perfected in Christ."[9] Irenaeus also taught that the Word of God imparted wisdom to the Greeks and to other peoples, which could be called "the Word's partial manifestation through human history."[10] In the words of Eusebius, this was "as a 'preparation for the Gospel' (*praeparatio evangelica*)."[11]

Origen was a learned teacher who articulated a vision of the spiritual transformation of the whole cosmos. God's love will eventually persuade all, even the devil, to repent and turn to God: "not even the tiniest sin will remain in the reign of the Father, and the word will be fulfilled that 'God will be all in all' (*Comm. In Io.* 1:32)."[12] In his Christian Platonism, he believed "that *evil is non-being* . . . [Evil] cannot exist forever."[13] Even punishment in the afterlife is not for retribution but for reformation. "Salvation will have to be voluntary, for all, by means of a conversion that will be enabled by the healing action of Christ . . . '*no being is incurable for the One who created it.*'"[14] Acts uses a word that will become a favorite term for Origen: "the time of universal restoration (*apokatastasis*) that God announced long ago through his holy prophets" (Acts 3:21). "Origen interprets the 'universal restoration' mentioned in Acts 3:20–21 as the 'perfect end' after all eons."[15]

There is quite a string of important church fathers who believe in the universal rectification and salvation of souls.

9. *Stromata* VII, 2 and I, 5, 3; quoted in Dupuis, *Toward Religious Pluralism*, 67.

10. Dupuis, *Toward Religious Pluralism*, 78.

11. Dupuis, *Toward Religious Pluralism*, 73.

12. This is the *Commentary on John 1:32*; quoted by Ramelli, *Larger Hope?*, 56.

13. Ramelli, *Larger Hope?*, 42–43, citing *Princ.* (*On First Principles*) 2:9:2; 1:7:5; *Comm. In Io.* (*Commentary on John*) 2:13.

14. Ramelli, *Larger Hope?*, 46, quoting *Princ.* 3:6:5.

15. Ramelli, *Larger Hope?*, 58, citing *Princ.* 2:3:5 and *Comm. In Matt.* (*Commentary on Matthew*) 17:19.

Methodius wrote, "The Logos assumed human nature in order to defeat the serpent and destroy the condemnation that arose with the fall of humanity . . . The law of the gospel, it alone, has saved all [*pantas*]."[16] For Eusebius, "after the Judgement there will come the 'rectification of all' and the vanishing of all adverse powers (2:4:13–4)."[17] "At the constitution of the new aeon, God will no longer inhabit few, but all . . . God will be 'all in all.'"[18] Of course, Eusebius is speaking of the afterlife here, as is Marcellus, when he affirms the "'restoration of all' and 'rectification of all.'"[19]

Athanasius talked about the whole world being led to God: "The Logos became a human being for the sake of our salvation [. . .] to set free all beings in himself, to lead the world to the Father and to pacify all beings in himself, in heaven and on earth."[20] He uses Isaiah to make a point about the universal spread of the gospel: "Now, unto all the earth has gone forth their voice, and all the earth has been filled with the knowledge of God [Isa 11:9], and the disciples have made disciples of all the nations [Matt 28:19], and now is fulfilled what is written, 'They shall be all taught of God'" [Isa 54:13; quoted in John 6:45].[21]

Gregory of Nyssa taught of a restoration of original purity to those who had sinned: "'the restoration of those who have fallen to their original condition.' . . . Gregory makes it clear that this restoration of the image of God depends on Christ and on divine grace."[22] Evil and sin cannot endure; "there will come a 'complete elimination of evil.'"[23] This leads us to the subject of *theōsis*, the

16. *Symp. (Symposium)* 3:6; 10:2; Ramelli, *Larger Hope?*, 71.

17. From *C. Marc (Against Marcellus of Ancyra)*; Ramelli, *Larger Hope?*, 77.

18. Eusebius, *Eccl. Theol. (The Theology of the Church)* 3:16; Ramelli, *Larger Hope?*, 78.

19. *Against Marcellus*; Ramelli, *Larger Hope?*, 86.

20. *Letter to Adelphius*, PG 26.1081. Quoted in Ramelli, *Larger Hope?*, 88.

21. Athanasius, *Fourth Discourse Against the Arians* I.13.59.8. From NPNF 2, vol. 4:879.

22. The quote is from *De hom. Op. (On the Creation of the Human Being)* 17; Ramelli, *Larger Hope?*, 118–19.

23. Quoting *In inscr. Ps. (On the Titles of the Psalms)* 101; Ramelli, *Larger Hope?*, 116.

divinization or deification of believers. Gregory believed "Only Christ allows the deification of humanity, because in him human nature is joined to the divinity: 'by participating in the purest being, human weakness is transformed into what is better and more powerful.'"[24] Of course, for most people this is an "otherworldly purification."[25] But the process can begin in this life. An important concept of Gregory's is "epektasis or constant progress . . . Gregory described the ideal of human perfection as constant progress in virtue and godliness . . . Humanity's goal is to become more and more perfect, more like God, even though humanity will never understand, much less attain, God's transcendence."[26]

Gregory's friend, Gregory of Nazianzen, is the one who actually coined the term *theōsis*. Beeley writes about *theōsis* in Gregory of Nazianzen: "Through the mixture of God with human existence in Christ, Christians are 'intertwined (*plakēnai*) with God and become God,' Gregory writes. Through the Incarnation we come to share in what is properly Christ's own, the divine nature, so that in the end 'God will be all in all' (1 Cor. 15:28) and we will be filled with God and him alone."[27] The effect will be worldwide: "'God will be all in all' [1 Cor 15:28] in the time of the restoration [*apokatastasis*] . . . We shall be all entirely conformed to God, able to receive God wholly, and God alone."[28] We can see the intersection of universalism and world repair in such sayings as Julian of Norwich's reference to: "the oneing of all mankind that shall be saved unto the blessed Trinity."[29]

It's not just the divinity, but the humanity of Christ that is essential to the incarnation's value for human beings. "If he is not like

---

24. Quoting *Orations against Eunomius* 3:4; Ramelli, *Larger Hope?*, 122.

25. Ramelli, *Larger Hope?*, 122.

26. OrthodoxWiki page on Gregory of Nyssa. https://orthodoxwiki.org/Gregory_of_Nyssa.

27. Beeley, "Christ and Human Flourishing," 138. He quotes Gregory of Nazianzen, *Oration* 30.3, 6.

28. Gregory of Nazianzen, *On the Son* (*Or.* 30:6); Ramelli, *Larger Hope?*, 133.

29. *Revelations of Divine Love*, 31; Ramelli, *Larger Hope?*, 209.

us in every way, one consequence is that we cannot be expected to be like him."[30] The incarnation was intended to bring divinity to humanity: "He became as we are that we might become as he is."[31]

Evagrius taught universal salvation: "If all nations will come and worship the Lord, then clearly also those who wage war will, and if this is the case, the whole nature of rational creatures will submit to the Name of the Lord."[32] Many of the church fathers argued against the idea that torment in the afterlife was everlasting. Rather, it was of limited duration, and for the purpose of purging the soul of evil. Theodore of Mopsuestia asks, "How can the resurrection be considered a grace, if those who are resurrected will be inflicted a punishment that does not result in a correction?"[33] Diodore prayed, "I realize that all of your scouring is aimed at correcting and improving a person."[34] Didymus the Blind wrote that "this fire of the corrective punishment is not active against the substance, but against [bad] habits and qualities."[35]

For most of the Greek fathers, the subject of the spiritual unification of humanity was mediated through the idea of universal salvation. Some of the Latin fathers, who did not support the idea of universal salvation, nevertheless drew upon some of the same themes.

Augustine firmly believed in infernalism, or the eternal punishment of souls in hell, yet he retained some of the ideas affirming God's corrective action. He touched upon the issue of Godly human community in his *City of God* and other works. He taught that "The Incarnation of Christ thus makes possible the union of all people in a single community of love . . . The City of God is the

30. Case-Winters, *God Will Be All*, 9.

31. Irenaeus, *Against Heresies* 5, preface; ANF 1:526; quoted in Case-Winters, *God Will Be All*, 15.

32. Evagrius, *KG (Chapters on Knowledge)* 6:27; Ramelli, *Larger Hope?*, 136.

33. A Latin fragment of Theodore of Mopsuestia preserved in PL 48:232; Ramelli, *Larger Hope?*, 143.

34. Diodore, *Commentary on Psalm* 39; Ramelli, *Larger Hope?*, 142.

35. Didymus the Blind, *Commentary on Psalm* 20–21; Ramelli, *Larger Hope?*, 96.

only true society."[36] Summarizing Augustine's argument in *De doctrina Christiana*, Beeley says that, for Augustine, "the love of God is the one thing that truly *enables* the love of self and neighbors."[37] "The City of God . . . will be constituted by the love of its citizens for God and for one another."[38] The true home of a Christian is in heaven, but some of that heavenly love can be brought down to earth and earthly society.

One of the most important works that deals with the idea of a perfected community is Augustine's *City of God*. Wherever and whenever the will of God is followed, there is the City of God; wherever selfish and sinful ends are pursued, that is the Earthly City. The City of God exists in heaven and on earth, but it is not identical with the church, since the latter is full of sinners and halfhearted believers. When it comes to peace and godliness, Augustine emphasizes orderliness. "Domestic peace has a relation to civic peace—in other words, that the well-ordered concord of domestic obedience and domestic rule has a relation to the well-ordered concord of civic obedience and civic rule."[39] He develops a very conservative social vision: "They who care for the rest rule—the husband the wife, the parents the children, the masters the servants; and they who are cared for obey—the women their husbands, the children their parents, the servants their masters."[40]

But he does articulate the principle of a truly interracial community of peace: "This heavenly city, then, while it sojourns on earth, calls citizens out of all nations, and gathers together a society of pilgrims of all languages, not scrupling about diversities in the manners, laws, and institutions whereby earthly peace is secured

36. Beeley, "Christ and Human Flourishing," 144. He is citing Augustine, *En. Ps. (Expositions on the Psalms)* 32, *exp.* 2.4; *De doctrina Christiana (On Christian Doctrine)* 1.39–41; *Civ. Dei (City of God)* 19.

37. Beeley, "Christ and Human Flourishing," 147.

38. Beeley, "Christ and Human Flourishing," 148. He is citing Augustine, *En. Ps.* 98.4.

39. Augustine, *City of God* XIX.16; Oates ed., 493.

40. Augustine, *City of God* XIX.14; Oates ed., 491.

and maintained."[41] There is no room for false or dishonest Christians. "Where there is no true religion there are no true virtues."[42]

Some of the most interesting defenders of the *theōsis* idea were Russian philosophers. Vladimir Soloviev and Evgenii Trubetskoi developed the idea of Bogochelovechestvo. "Bogochelovechestvo refers to the free human realization of the divine principle in ourselves and in the world, to the realization of humanity's intrinsic divine potential—deification or, to use the patristic term, *theōsis*. It is the divine-human project of building the kingdom of God and of cosmic transformation in the unity of all (*vseedinstvo*), in which God will be all in all (1 Cor 15:28)."[43] Again we encounter this key unity-affirming Scripture. Trubetskoi taught that "The Christian ideal requires the perfect reconciliation of human freedom with Divine grace in Christ—the organic unity and interaction of free Divinity and free humanity."[44]

In his St. Petersburg lectures, Soloviev developed the idea of Christ perfecting the human race. "There is the unity that produces and the unity that is produced . . . In the divine organism of Christ, the acting, unifying principle . . . is . . . Logos. The second kind of unity, the produced unity, is called Sophia."[45] "Sophia is ideal or perfect humanity, eternally contained in the integral divine being, or Christ."[46] Sophia is "the world soul, or ideal humanity."[47] "In being determined or formed by the divine Logos, the world soul enables the Holy Spirit to actualize itself in the all . . . The world soul can communicate the divine all-unity to all of creation only insofar as it itself is permeated by that unity . . . by the power of Divinity present in it."[48] "Mankind has to *co-operate* with God in

41. Augustine, *City of God* XIX.17; Oates ed., 494.

42. Augustine, *City of God* XIX.25; Oates ed., 504.

43. Poole, "Evgenii Trubetskoi and Russian Liberal Theology," 31.

44. Poole, "Evgenii Trubetskoi and Russian Liberal Theology," 35, quoting an untranslated work.

45. Soloviev ("Solovyov"), *Lectures*, 107–8.

46. Soloviev ("Solovyov"), *Lectures*, 113.

47. Soloviev ("Solovyov"), *Lectures*, 131.

48. Soloviev ("Solovyov"), *Lectures*, 132.

this work, for otherwise there cannot be a complete oneing of God with his creatures and a full expression of the meaning of existence, which requires not a mere coming-together but the concord and unity of all."[49]

THE LOVE OF GOD

A primary principle through all periods of Christian thought is love, due to the preeminence of love in the teachings and practice of Jesus, something that the church is expected to put into practice. We can start with gratitude for the good news that we are loved by God. We can then make that an invitation to others to recognize the spiritual over-care of God, and the spiritual kinship of all members of the family of God. We testify that the Son of the living God is the head of this family.

Jesus wants us to be part of his great family. He illuminated what was possible in a human relationship with God. When we study Jesus, we study what is possible for our faith walk, the generosity, forgiveness, and integrity that *we* can practice, the peace and harmony *we* can experience. He wants to help us to socialize, to study, and to grow, always learning about the Living God. Which of our life experiences can we share with the Son of the living God? All of them. He cares about all of us. He has already walked *with* us every step of the way. He is still walking with us.

The hymn "Come, Christians, Join to Sing" says "He is our guide and friend; to us he'll condescend; his love shall never end."[50] Jesus showed us how to love. He taught the apostles to love even their enemies (Matt 5:44). Love can be persuasive when it is surprising, as when offering to carry a soldier's pack a second mile if compelled to carry it one mile (Matt 5:41). Imagine the soldier's surprise upon hearing this. Jesus practiced this love. He healed the servant of a Roman centurion, while praising the centurion's faith (Matt 8:5–13). Compassion was his characteristic feature. Even on

---

49. Soloviev ("Solovyev"), *God, Man and the Church*, 134.
50. Bateman and DeBruyn, "Come, Christians, Join to Sing."

the cross, he said "Father, forgive them; for they do not know what they are doing" (Luke 23:34).

And he sought for unity among his followers. "I ask . . . that they may all be one. As you, Father, are in me and I am in you, may they also be in us, so that the world may believe that you have sent me" (John 17:20–21). We have seen that he took his apostles into predominantly Gentile regions, and that he expressed openness to many Gentiles who approached him. A Canaanite woman was a bit sassy in her response to Jesus, yet he was moved to say "Woman, great is your faith! Let it be done for you as you wish" and to heal her daughter (Matt 15:27–28).

Jesus pictures the loving care of God in the parable of the prodigal son, in which he shows a father pouring love upon a wandering son. John Sanders sees this parable as highlighting the contrast between Authoritative, Permissive, and Nurturant models of parenting. Jesus uses the prodigal son parable to show how different those models are. An Authoritative father would not simply accept his wandering son back, but would rebuke the son and demand that he earn his way back into good graces. An Authoritative father demands that every child gets what he deserves. And the hearers of the parable might expect that, too. But the father in Jesus' parable does not do that. He welcomes back the son with joy, as though finding a lost son or one who was rescued from "a life-threatening condition . . . God does not demand repayment or punishment in order to bestow divine acceptance."[51] Nor is this a permissive approach that cares nothing about the son's behavior. The father *does* say that the son has been "dead" and "lost"; he never says that the son's behavior does not matter. He just insists on using love instead of punishment or a demand for penance to reintegrate the younger son into the family. Sanders says there are both Nurturant and Authoritative texts in the OT. Jesus clearly chose the Nurturant approach and ignored most of the Authoritative passages.[52] Leviticus shows a nurturant attitude when it says "love the alien as yourself" (Lev 19:34). And Deuteronomy says

51. Sanders, *Embracing Prodigals*, xii.
52. Sanders, *Embracing Prodigals*, xv.

"You shall also love the stranger, for you were strangers in the land of Egypt" (10:19).[53] Further, "Nurturant and Authoritative types are found in most religions."[54] I would have chosen the word "authoritarian" rather than "Authoritative," for the latter word, to me, signifies something that is respectable for good reasons. I think Sanders really means "authoritarian" when he says "Authoritative." I agree with his point that choosing Jesus entails choosing the Nurturant approach.

The unity of the family of God needs the love of the nurturing Father. Every community is shaped by its understanding of the *qualities* of God. Jesus wanted his followers to feel included, like members of a family sitting together at a table. "You may eat and drink at my table in my kingdom" (Luke 22:30). He wants us to feel at home in his community, and not to feel like we have to be content with scraps. "Fear not, little flock; it is the Father's good pleasure to give you the kingdom" (Luke 12:32). We have a place at Christ's table, in the family of God. Sanders cites numerous studies showing that those with a Nurturing God concept "are more cooperative, agreeable, and have better social relationships" than those with an Authoritative concept; they have higher self-esteem and treat their significant others better.[55]

There is also an imperative that we learn to listen with compassionate interest to those whose political beliefs differ from our own. "Develop personal relationships of mutual understanding and trust with those with whom you have political disagreements."[56] There can be no civil dialogue if people do not make an effort to understand the beliefs of others. The real secret for success in such conversations is "that rare combination of deep commitment to their own beliefs with openness to respectfully listen and then talk with other Christians who are deeply committed to a differing set of beliefs."[57]

53. Sanders, *Embracing Prodigals*, 33.

54. Sanders, *Embracing Prodigals*, xvii.

55. Sanders, *Embracing Prodigals*, 42–43.

56. Heie, *Let's Talk*, 43.

57. Heie, *Let's Talk*, 66.

Harold Heie has devoted decades to encouraging respectful dialogue between people of differing viewpoints. He formed a project called the Respectful Conversations Project with a website at respectfulconversation.net, and has hosted a number of large-scale online conversations on evangelicalism, human sexuality, and political discourse.[58] One of the results of his efforts is that people came away with an increased appreciation for the viewpoints and experiences of those with whom they disagreed. Not many people changed their opinions on the issues, but many of them changed their understanding of, and ability to converse with, those with whom they disagreed.[59]

Responding to Jesus' prayer in John 17, David Drum writes, "Jesus was praying specifically for His followers, not for political parties, and His prayer was not that we come to agreement on philosophies, political or otherwise, but that we love one another. Love implies listening, respect, humility, service."[60] Our identity in Christ is the main thing, and it is the only thing that conveys inner peace and meaning.[61] If we place our identity in our political party loyalties, we are sunk. "Any time we place our identity in anything secondary, tragedy results."[62] That tragedy is conflict, blame, and misunderstanding of others.

TOWARDS CHRISTIAN UNITY

Efforts toward unity, or at least understanding and mutual love, have been growing within Christian communities. In the 1990s, some church leaders realized that their efforts were not breaking any new ground, and that large groups, mostly evangelical and Pentecostal churches, were not part of the ecumenical effort, and were not interested in joining. But they *were* interested in becoming

58. Heie, *Let's Talk*, 70.
59. Heie, *Let's Talk*, 78.
60. Drum, *Peace Talks*, 203.
61. Drum, *Peace Talks*, 92.
62. Drum, *Peace Talks*, 73.

part of a conversation. Large meetings were held in Pasadena in 2000 and 2002, which brought together members of those groups as well as Lutheran, Catholic, and Orthodox churches.

The meetings had an emphasis on sharing personal stories. "There was deep and challenging listening between everyone . . . Encouragement and joy really did overflow at this 'discovery' of brothers and sisters in the faith, which allowed people better to 'hear' the uniqueness of each tradition on its own terms."[63] This group, the Global Christian Forum, had its First Global Gathering in 2007 in Limuru. There was a widespread perception of a need for a revisioning of Christian unity and discussion. Some groups admitted to having contributed to disunity through pride: "How many of our divisions and tensions can be traced back to a failure to act toward one another with humility and gentleness, to a lack of patience and love for one another? . . . We share a common *hope* . . . We all profess *one Lord* and Saviour . . . Every church is called to be an instrument of God's grace."[64]

Further regional meetings have extended the Global Christian Forum's reach into Europe, Africa, Latin America, and East Asia. Another global gathering was held in Manado in 2012, with participants coming from sixty-five countries.[65] The meeting developed theological principles. The Third Global Gathering took place in Bogota in 2018. This group seeks Christian unity and is not organizationally committed to achieving unity and understanding with non-Christian religions. But some members have hopes in that direction. A Syrian Chaldean bishop writes:

> The Second Vatican Council . . . prompted Christians and all members of the church to consider their presence in the Arab and Muslim world as a *dynamic of communion.* Such a dynamic is to be sought first between Christians, then between Christians and Muslims . . . At the very heart of present-day Syrian society and in the middle of raging violence, all Christians have displayed

63. Rowland Jones, "Global Christian Forum," in *Revisioning*, 8.
64. Michel, "Bible Studies," 107.
65. Rowland Jones, "Global Christian Forum," in *Transformation*, 235.

a remarkable example of solidarity and stewardship towards the poorest without any discrimination whatsoever, thus drawing the attention of the Muslims and stirring up questions on their part as to the Christian faith![66]

Christian unity is an important step toward world unity. "The most creative social strategy we have to offer is the church. Here we show the world a manner of life the world can never achieve through social coercion or government action."[67]

What is really practical, as regards spiritual unity among those who think differently? What really matter are the right attitudes, the willingness to respect the spiritual commitments of others. The usefulness of any concrete, organizational steps that are taken is entirely dependent on approaching the process with the right attitude and insight. True unity is not an institutional product, but a spiritual one. Therefore I do not suggest any institutional steps, but only the principles. If we have the right principles, institutional steps will follow, and they will be helpful to the degree that they follow the Christly attitude and principle.

TEILHARD'S PHILOSOPHY

The twentieth-century philosopher, Pierre Teilhard de Chardin, posited Christ as the starting point, the organizer, and the endpoint of evolution. He is taking the biblical and patristic principle of Christ as life-giver and interweaving it with the scientific idea of evolution. To be relevant in an age of science, theology needs to "come to grips with science, in general, and evolution, in particular."[68]

As a geologist and paleontologist, Teilhard studied evolution. He came to claim that evolution proceeded meaningfully in a direction of increasing complexity. Evolution was not simply random.

66. Audo, "Reflections," 175–76.
67. Hauerwas and Willimon, *Resident Aliens*, 82–83.
68. Haught, *Cosmic Vision of Teilhard*, 77.

The increasing complexity of molecules was *meant* to produce life; the increasing complexity of life was meant to produce humanity; and the increasing complexity of human life is meant to produce, in the end, spiritual unity. As the theologian John Haught put it: "Matter historically prepares the way for the appearance of life, life for mind, and mind for spirit."[69] "The cosmos is a promise that remains to be fulfilled."[70]

In Teilhard's own words: "We can progress only by uniting: this, as we have seen, is the law of Life. But unification through coercion leads only to a superficial pseudo-unity . . . Therefore it is inwardly that we must come together, and in entire freedom. . . . such as can only be realised in a universal, mutual love . . . This majestic process . . . can achieve its consummation only in becoming Christianised."[71] Although the Vatican forbade his publishing during his lifetime, he never stopped writing, and his posthumously published works have had a wide effect, including having a major effect on Vatican II.[72]

Teilhard argued that Christ is the active agent in the evolutionary field: "the human layer of the earth is wholly and continuously under the organizing influx of the incarnate Christ."[73] This is how he understood such passages as this one: "Christ is all and in all" (Col 3:11). Christ is deeply involved in human history: "The kingdom of God is within us. When Christ appears in the clouds he will simply be manifesting a metamorphosis that has been slowly accomplished under his influence in the heart of the mass of mankind."[74] A pair of scholars summarize Teilhard's view thus: "Christ . . . is himself the *cause and center* of evolution and its goal. This evolutive Christ is not distinct from Jesus but is indeed 'Jesus,

---

69. Haught, *John Haught Reader*, 258.

70. Haught, *Cosmic Vision of Teilhard*, 10.

71. Teilhard de Chardin, "Some Reflections on Progress," in *Future of Man*, 74–76.

72. Haught, *Cosmic Vision of Teilhard*, 76.

73. Teilhard de Chardin, *Divine Milieu*, 124.

74. Teilhard de Chardin, *Divine Milieu*, 128.

the center towards whom all moves.'"[75] Teilhard insisted that Christ is related *organically* to humanity, not just juridically, as a heavenly Judge.

Other religions will eventually converge with the religion of Christ: "[Teilhard] described the emergence of Christ as 'a general convergence of religions upon a universal personal center of unity who fundamentally satisfies them all.'"[76] One of his basic principles is that Christ is the Omega Point, the goal, of all human evolution. World evolution focalizes as human evolution, which culminates in transformation into Christlikeness: "Cosmogenesis, proceeding along an axis of anthropogenesis, culminates in a Christogenesis."[77]

Teilhard would say he was simply recognizing certain fundamental truths: "In the nature of things everything that is faith must rise, and everything that rises must converge."[78] There is an imperative that we become actively involved in the world. "We are called to love this created world as God loves it."[79] By so doing, we actually contribute to God's work. "What Teilhard tried to show is that evolution in all its materiality is not only the universe coming to be but it is *God* who is coming to be. Thus he states, 'God is entirely self-sufficient; and yet the universe contributes *something that is vitally necessary to* God.'"[80] Christ's consciousness will preside over the cosmos: "Physically and literally, he is he who *consummates*: the plenitude of the world being finally effected only in the final synthesis in which a supreme consciousness will appear upon total, supremely organized, complexity."[81]

75. Dinges and Delio, "Teilhard de Chardin and the New Spirituality," 174; quoting De Lubac, *Pierre Teilhard*, 37.

76. Delio, "Evolution and the Rise of the Secular God" 37; she quotes Teilhard, *Christianity and Evolution*, 130.

77. Teilhard de Chardin, "My Fundamental Vision," in *Toward the Future*, 204.

78. Teilhard de Chardin, "Faith in Man," in *Future of Man*, 192.

79. Dinges and Delio, "Teilhard de Chardin and the New Spirituality," 177.

80. Dinges and Delio, "Teilhard de Chardin and the New Spirituality," quoting Teilhard de Chardin, *Christianity and Evolution*, 177.

81. Teilhard de Chardin, *Let Me Explain*, 101; original source, *Science and Christ*, 166.

Building on the thought of Teilhard, and considering the influence of world religions like Hinduism, Buddhism, Jainism, Zoroastrianism, and others, John Haught argues, "Religion is a gradual but grateful awakening to the elusive horizon of unrestricted being, goodness, truth, and beauty. These are 'transcendental' ideals that, for the sake of linguistic economy, I refer to collectively as rightness."[82] He speaks of humanity striving for transcendence and rightness. "The quest for religious unity in an unfinished universe begins with the shared anticipation of a transcendent rightness that is both real and waiting to be realized."[83] Striving and waiting are essential parts of religious living.

Our work here is supremely important. Teilhard saw us as "building the world" in partnership with God. "We are spiritualized by being carried along by the spiritualization of all things. We are united to Christ by entering into communion with all men."[84] As we work together, we "achieve a wider degree of freedom," even "*the triumph of freedom*."[85]

Some theologians thought Teilhard put too much faith in science and in evolution, and needed to do more to affirm traditional doctrines. But listen to his own words: "The essence of Christianity is neither more nor less than a belief in the unification of the world in God by the Incarnation."[86] And again: "Christ would not be the sole Mover, the sole Issue, of the Universe if it were possible for the Universe in any way to integrate itself, even to a lesser degree, apart from Christ . . . It is therefore towards Christ, in fact, that we turn our eyes when, however approximate our concept of it may be, we look ahead towards a higher pole of humanization and personalization."[87]

---

82. Haught, *New Cosmic Story*, 28.

83. Haught, *New Cosmic Story*, 110.

84. Teilhard de Chardin, *Science and Christ*, 77; quoted in Vacek, "Evolving Christian Morality," 158.

85. Teilhard de Chardin, "Formation," in *Future of Man*, 182–83.

86. Teilhard de Chardin, *Let Me Explain*, 99; original source, *Human Energy*, 91–92.

87. Teilhard de Chardin, *Let Me Explain*, 100; original source, *Science and*

Christ is causative. I see a similar point in the early twentieth-century writer Peter Forsyth: "[Christ] is not a product of man's spiritual evolution but its grand source . . . The King makes the Kingdom and not the Kingdom the King."[88]

Teilhard promises that his method does not lead to pantheism. "This figure of the Universal Christ, the prime mover, the savior, the master and the term of what our age calls evolution, entails no risk, we should note, of the disappearance of the man-Christ, or of a deviation of mysticism into some pantheistic and impersonal form of worship. The Universal Christ, born from an expansion of the heart of Jesus, requires the historical reality of his human nature if he is not to disappear."[89] Teilhard had an intense dialogue with pantheism; he felt drawn toward pantheism, toward the presence of the divine in nature, but he rejected as false those Eastern types of mysticism that saw the self being absorbed and disappearing into the All; he advocated for Western types of mysticism in which there was a process of the "Absolute . . . gathering up of all beings into itself, maintaining their difference whilst uniting them. This implies a higher degree of consciousness and a progressive personalization."[90]

Somewhat unfortunately, Teilhard chose to use the terms "the road of the East" and the "road of the West" to distinguish a mystical approach that attempted to "escape from matter" and involved a "draining away of self," from an approach that sought the "transformation of matter" and "a higher form of personalization."[91] Nevertheless, he spoke highly of the "so human figure of Amida" in Chinese Buddhism.[92] Essential to a mature and healthy mysticism was "the maintenance of the primacy of the *spirit* over

Christ, 165.

88. Forsyth, *Person and Place of Jesus Christ*, 333–34.

89. Teilhard de Chardin, "Awaited Word," in *Toward the Future*, 99.

90. King, *Towards a New Mysticism*, 121.

91. King, *Towards a New Mysticism*, 127, 129–30.

92. Teilhard de Chardin, "Spiritual Contribution," in *Toward the Future*, 136.

matter" and "the primacy in the spiritual of the *personal*."[93] Teilhard's philosophy might have benefitted from drawing on the personalist philosophies of Borden Parker Bowne and Max Scheler, but he seems to not have known about those authors, though he did have a "remarkable convergence with" the French personalist Emmanuel Mounier.[94]

Both Mounier and Teilhard affirmed freedom, but it is not an absolute freedom. Teilhard understood freedom as "the possibility of maturing . . . Authentic freedom is fidelity to self, to a self purified, in a word, fidelity to love."[95]

Teilhard shows his personalist viewpoint when he argues that greater unity does not obliterate individuality, does not impose a "hive," just the opposite: "*true union* (that is to say, synthesis) does not confound; it differentiates . . . far from giving birth to a mere mechanism . . . Anarchic autonomy tends to disappear, but it does so in order to achieve its consummation in the harmonised flowering of individual values."[96] Cosmic unification involves and affirms complexity and uniqueness. "Only union *through* love and *in* love . . . can physically possess the property of not merely differentiating but also personalising the elements which comprise it . . . Mankind will only find and shape itself if men can learn to love one another in the very act of drawing closer."[97] Bowne affirms this point: "Both love and religion seek for union, but it is not the union of absorption or fusion, but rather the union of mutual understanding and sympathy."[98]

Teilhard engaged in interfaith discussions in the mid-twentieth century, especially in connection with the World Congress of Faiths. He did not "proclaim the essential sameness of all religions,"

---

93. Teilhard de Chardin, "Spiritual Contribution," 132; she is quoting "Road of the West" in *Towards the Future*, 54.

94. Ligneul, *Teilhard and Personalism*, 6.

95. Ligneul, *Teilhard and Personalism*, 19–20.

96. Teilhard de Chardin, "Grand Option," in *Future of Man*, 53–54.

97. Teilhard de Chardin, "Directions and Conditions," in *Future of Man*, 235.

98. Bowne, *Personalism*, 284.

but called for bringing "closer together all those who believe in a future for man and the world," and argued that these human efforts toward understanding required "the central insights of the great religious traditions" to "find their true centre."[99]

Further, "Christ is still the only cosmic element we can see that can . . . give a body to modern hopes for a spiritual organization of the world."[100] He frequently mentioned an anticipated "convergence of religions,"[101] but rarely spelled out exactly what that meant. He thought that world religions could contribute something to the convergence, if they retain "a personalistic form of love."[102] He wrote of "a general convergence of religions upon a universal Christ who fundamentally satisfies them all: that seems to be the only possible conversion of the world."[103] He spoke of a new mysticism, one that involves "the integration of the love of God with the love of the world,"[104] even a "love of evolution."[105] This new mysticism, King says, "can only become a reality insofar as others go beyond [Teilhard] in exploring this new path."[106] Teilhard marked the beginning, not the end, of this cosmic philosophizing.

Teilhard had a highly developed idea of Christ, but did not have a very developed idea of the Spirit, tending to simply conflate the Spirit to Christ. Neville astutely observes: "the confusion of *Christ* and *Spirit* is the result of inattention on Teilhard's part to the problem of God's transcendence and immanence in relation to evolution."[107] Further, there are points at which Teilhard's evo-

---

99. King, *Towards a New Mysticism*, 92.

100. Teilhard de Chardin, *Toward the Future*, 55.

101. King, *Towards a New Mysticism*, 159.

102. Quoted by C. Cuénot in *Etudes Teilhardiennes* 1 (1968) 57; quoted in King, *Towards a New Mysticism*, 208.

103. Teilhard de Chardin, *Christianity and Evolution*, 130; quoted in King, *Towards a New Mysticism*, 162.

104. King, *Towards a New Mysticism*, 202.

105. Teilhard de Chardin, *Christianity and Evolution*, 183; quoted in King, *Towards a New Mysticism*, 207.

106. King, *Towards a New Mysticism*, 218.

107. Neville, "Nine Books," 82n37.

lutionary theory seems like a new dogma with its continual appeal to the abstract idea of evolution. "Does not the focus on earthly evolution obscure the concrete significance of the events of human history?"[108] Further, although Teilhard believed in free will, should he not have put more emphasis on it, on the *choice* that is required for human participation with the divine?

I think Teilhard sometimes failed to make a necessary distinction between matter and spirit. In his enthusiasm to see spirit operative in evolution and in humanity, he treated matter as though it *were* spirit: "There is neither spirit nor matter in the world; the stuff of the universe is spirit-matter."[109]

One theologian who was inspired by Teilhard's ideas, without actually following his method, was Karl Rahner. Rahner was not interested in following Teilhard's "attempt at a full integration of science and theology."[110] He liked Teilhard's idea of Christ as "Omega Point," but thought it needed to be tied more closely "with Jesus of Nazareth."[111] Rahner retains the idea that science and theology are distinct, resisting any "attempt at the kind of full integration that Teilhard undertakes."[112] With teachings that resembled those of the church fathers, Rahner emphasized the transformative function of the resurrection, which is "the beginning of the transformation of the world . . . Theology might then show why Jesus as pledge and beginning of the perfect fulfilment of the world, as representative of the new cosmos, as dispenser of the Spirit . . . can only be fully grasped if he is known throughout as the risen Lord."[113]

Rahner articulated a strongly anti-authoritarian value system. He said "ideology is then a fundamental closure in face of

108. Neville, "Nine Books," 82.

109. Teilhard de Chardin, *Human Energy*, 57–58; quoted by Haughey, "Teilhard," 213.

110. Edwards, "Teilhard's Vision," 57.

111. Edwards, "Teilhard's Vision," 57.

112. Edwards, "Teilhard's Vision," 58.

113. Rahner, "Resurrection: D. Theology," 1442. Quoted in Edwards, "Teilhard's Vision," 62.

the 'wholeness' of reality, one which turns a partial aspect into an absolute . . . and thus usually takes the form of a basic determination of political activity . . . Christianity is not an ideology."[114]

Both Teilhard and Rahner are close to the Greek church fathers in their retention of the biblical principle of Christ as creator and as sponsor of human transformation. I have argued that Christ's saving work is the *same* as his creating work. As he healed people, he saved them. As he forgave their sins, he restored their self-respect. Healing and saving both involve life-giving. His saving power is the same life-giving principle as his healing and his creator power.[115]

Teilhard is reshaping a patristic point when he argues that Jesus is the designer and guide of evolution itself. Jesus is the father of biological life and the sponsor of spiritual growth. Insofar as he carries out divine creativity in the realm of time and space, Jesus is *God-in-Time*. His sovereign power overlaps with his life-giving ministry. He is transforming us "by the power that also enables him to make all things subject to himself" (Phil 3:21). In the end, Jesus "hands over the kingdom to God the Father . . . When all things are subjected to him, then the Son himself will also be subjected to the one who put all things in subjection under him, so that God may be all in all" (1 Cor 15:24, 28). As we take part in this, the body of Christ "increaseth with the increase of God" (Col 2:19 ASV). As we grow spiritually, God-in-Time grows in universe power through us. Our progress, both here and hereafter, helps to perfect the universe. "The path of the just is like the shining sun, that shines ever brighter unto the perfect day" (Prov 4:18 NKJV).

Evolution encourages survival of the fittest, but in philosophy this means *survival of the truest* (in the long run). Whether individually or collectively, indifference to truth is fatal. "In the long run" is a crucial article of faith, a trust in the justice of God beyond what we can see, and a repudiation of coercion as a means of promoting truth.

---

114. Rahner, "Ideology and Christianity," in *Rahner Reader*, 338, 341. Originally from *Theological Investigations VI*.

115. Finlan, *Salvation Not Purchased*, 83–85.

We get a glimpse of Teilhard's passionate heart when we read: "A few days before his death, Teilhard wrote: 'the truth need appear but once in one mind. Nothing can then prevent it from invading everything and inflaming everything.'"[116]

THE SPIRIT IN EVOLUTION

Some recent writing offers a potential update and corrective to Teilhard's philosophy. Denis Edwards wrote a book that emphasizes the role of the Spirit in creation, evolution, the incarnation, salvation, and transformation, although he never mentions Teilhard. But he seems to make the Teilhardian point while using Spirit-language: "The Spirit of God brooded over our universe from the very beginning as the Creator Spirit, the Breath of Life for all things. Creatures exist only because God gives them the 'breath of life' (Gen. 2:7 . . . 7:15)."[117] The Spirit is "the immanent Life-Giver that enables all creatures to be and to become."[118] The Spirit, then, is the life-giving force within creation. "The Spirit of God is at work in evolutionary emergence whenever something radically new occurs."[119] "The Spirit is to be seen as Creator and Life-Giver, not just in the sense of biological life but in the wider sense of being the one who brings a universe to life."[120] Of course, all three Persons of the Trinity are involved in the Creation, yet all the Persons have "distinct and proper roles."[121] The Father is "the Unoriginate Origin of everything"; the Son is "the Word/Wisdom of God as the *exemplar* and *image* for all creatures . . . the *icon of God* in whom 'all things' were created (Col. 1:15)"; the Spirit "is revealed as the Breath of God . . . that breathes life into creation, grace, incarnation, and church . . . the indwelling creative principle,

---

116. Ligneul, *Teilhard and Personalism*, 81.

117. Edwards, *Breath of Life*, 171–72.

118. Edwards, *Breath of Life*, 117.

119. Edwards, *Breath of Life*, 139.

120. Edwards, *Breath of Life*, 118.

121. Edwards, *Breath of Life*, 125.

permeating and filling the whole universe."[122] Quoting Moltmann, Edwards says "the Spirit is the 'unspeakable closeness of God.'"[123] Such insights lead not to pantheism but to *panentheism*—a word that comes from the Greek and means 'all things in God.'"[124] Steve McIntosh says he is a panentheist because "I recognize spirit as both immanent and transcendent."[125]

The Spirit is deeply involved with all life. Against the patristic emphasis on God's supposed impassivity, "it is important to be able to say that the Spirit of God suffers with suffering creation."[126] And "God's empathy and suffering with others are not to be thought of as diminishing God's transcendence."[127]

Rahner says "Christ is present and operative in . . . non-Christian religions in and through his *Spirit*."[128] That does not mean that the Spirit is diffuse and aimless. Edwards affirms Rahner's point "that the Spirit who is at work in grace throughout human history is always the Spirit directed toward Christ . . . The Spirit is oriented toward God's explicit self-giving in Christ."[129] Nevertheless, the Spirit may speak through other religions sometimes, so we should be open to other religions: "The Spirit of God may be addressing the Christian community in a prophetic way from another religious tradition."[130]

Relying on Yves Congar, Edwards insists that "needed are a theory and practice of church that involve a mutual and reciprocal relationship between Word and Spirit."[131] Too much emphasis on Word can lead to overemphasis on structure, and "may run the risk of becoming authoritarian"; too much emphasis on Spirit can

122. Edwards, *Breath of Life*, 126–27.

123. Edwards, *Breath of Life*, 128; Moltmann, *Spirit of Life*, 12.

124. McIntosh, *Evolution's Purpose*, 130.

125. McIntosh, *Evolution's Purpose*, xxiv.

126. Edwards, *Breath of Life*, 114.

127. Edwards, *Breath of Life*, 113.

128. Rahner, *Foundations of Christian Faith*, 316.

129. Edwards, *Breath of Life*, 57.

130. Edwards, *Breath of Life*, 63.

131. Edwards, *Breath of Life*, 92.

lead to individualism and losing "sight of the value of the Christian tradition."[132]

Edwards draws heavily on patristic sources. Irenaeus "liked to speak of God creating *with two hands*, that of the Word and that of the Spirit. He says, for example, that humanity 'having been molded at the beginning *by the hands of God*, that is, of the Son and the Spirit, is made after the image and likeness of God.'"[133] Irenaeus is drawing on Psalm 33:6: "By the word of the Lord the heavens were made, and all their host by the breath of his mouth."[134] God creates with his Word and Breath. Similarly, Athanasius thinks "of God as creating *through* the Word and *in* the Spirit."[135] Edwards especially relies on the reasoning of Basil the Great, who argued that the persons of the Trinity are always "indivisibly united . . . the divine persons act in communion."[136] "God exists as a Communion of Persons . . . this suggests that reality is relational to the core. It suggests a relational ontology—the very *being* of things is relational being."[137]

That is an insight that coincides with one of the fundamental principles of Process Theology.

PROCESS THEOLOGY AND PERSONALISM

Alfred North Whitehead is the founder of Process Philosophy, which enjoys considerable attention in academic theological circles today. This philosophy developed independently of Teilhard's, but overlaps it in time of origin. Its advocates today vary immensely, but they all share a hope for an intersection of forces leading toward integration and peace.

132. Edwards, *Breath of Life*, 93.

133. Edwards, *Breath of Life*, 40, quoting Irenaeus, *Against Heresies* 5.28.4.

134. Edwards, *Breath of Life*, 39; see Irenaeus, *Against Heresies* 1.22.1; 2.30.9.

135. Edwards, *Breath of Life*, 44.

136. Edwards, *Breath of Life*, 41, drawing on Basil's *On the Holy Spirit* 16.37.

137. Edwards, *Breath of Life*, 132.

The philosophy seems to begin with the insight that reality is dynamic, not static. Reality is processes and experiences, rather than independent *things*. "To be *actual* is to be a process."[138] "The Biblical tradition . . . does not support the extreme individualism of the modern Western world. In it, God is not viewed as devoid of relations to the world, and in human existence primary importance is given to one's relations with God and other humans . . . Process thought supports the relational, communal thrust of the Biblical view of God and humanity."[139]

Whitehead paid attention to values, which will shape the kind of world we will live in. He wrote, "A society is to be termed civilized whose members participate in the five qualities—Truth, Beauty, Adventure, Art, Peace."[140] But every good ideal has a way of degenerating into a harmful distortion. The enemy, Whitehead says, is "the doctrine of dogmatic finality," which can occur in science as well as in religion or philosophy.[141] Creativity and freshness need to be renewed in every generation.

Whitehead sees one of the biggest theological problems being the idea of a tyrannical God. "The notion of the absolute despot has stood in the way."[142] There is a "mischief which follows from banishing novelty, from trying to formularize your truth, from setting up to declare: 'This is all there is to be known on the subject, and discussion is closed.'"[143] This has led to bad theology "from Augustine, even in Francis of Assisi; the gentleness and mercy of one side of Christianity, but based logically on the most appalling system of concepts. The old ferocious God is back, the Oriental despot, the Pharaoh . . . with everything to enforce obedience, from infant damnation to eternal punishment."[144]

---

138. Cobb and Griffin, *Process Theology*, 14.

139. Cobb and Griffin, *Process Theology*, 22.

140. Whitehead, *Adventures of Ideas*, 283.

141. Whitehead, *Adventures of Ideas*, 166.

142. Whitehead, *Adventures of Ideas*, 174.

143. Whitehead and Price, *Dialogues of Alfred North Whitehead*, 145.

144. Whitehead and Price, *Dialogues of Alfred North Whitehead*, 144.

Process Theology repudiates the notion of coercive power, preferring to speak of God's persuasive power. Whitehead said God is "the fellow sufferer who understands."[145] "God's creative activity is persuasive, not controlling, it is a love that takes risks."[146]

Charles Hartshorne took Process Philosophy and developed it into Process Theology, placing a particular emphasis upon "a profound relativity of God,"[147] which means a profound *relatedness*. He finds the old idea of God as independent and impassive to be repulsive and illogical. We would not admire a king who was "independent, insensitive, ignorant, apathetic, nonrelative, toward what goes on in the hearts of men,"[148] nor should we imagine that of God. The notion of God as unfeeling and nonrelative is really a "worship of mere power or absoluteness."[149] Process Theology emphasizes a dynamic relationship between God and the world, with each influencing the other. God's knowledge of the world actually grows. Hartshorne insists "we are not obliterating the uniqueness of deity by affirming his relativity."[150]

Hartshorne affirmed the noncoercive principle: "God's influence is supreme . . . But the direct influence of God is analogous only to the direct power of thought over thought, and of feeling over feeling, and this is the power of inspiration or suggestion."[151]

I see Process Theology as a likely ally in the effort to achieve advanced concepts of spiritual progress, and to bring about interreligious peace. Its main drawback, to my way of thinking, is not what it affirms but what it denies, at least what one version of Process Theology denies. In seeking to emphasize process and relationship, Cobb and Griffin claim that certain traditional ideas need to be repudiated, such as "God as Cosmic Moralist" and "God

145. Whitehead, *Process and Reality*, 351.

146. Cobb and Griffin, *Process Theology*, 57.

147. Hartshorne, *Divine Relativity*, 24.

148. Hartshorne, *Divine Relativity*, 51.

149. Hartshorne, *Divine Relativity*, 52.

150. Hartshorne, *Divine Relativity*, 82.

151. Hartshorne, *Reality*, 275; quoted by Case-Winters, *God Will Be All*, 194.

as Controlling Power."[152] One can see that their main objection is to a rigid and heartless moralism and to a theology that sees God as responsible for everything that happens. One can share their resistance to these distortions without rejecting the idea that God is the ultimate lawgiver and that the infinite God is ultimately in control. Process Theology needs to find ways to allow the existence of the infinite God while also affirming its assertion of what I call God-in-Time: God in relationship with events in the time-space universe. Eternity's God is the Absolute, the "Alpha"; time's God is the Evolver, the "Omega."

Actually, Cobb and Griffin have some very useful things to say about the function of God-in-Time. They write, "Creative transformation is the essence of growth . . . The source of the novelty is the Logos, whose incarnation is Christ. Where Christ is effectively present, there is creative transformation . . . Christ is the giver of both responsive and creative human love."[153] Jesus encourages real transformation in people and systems: "The supreme gift is Peace, which is an alignment of ourselves with God's grace. . . . Peace is the gift of Christ and the fruit of the Spirit."[154] Process Theology also opens to door to a more responsible ecological consciousness. It "calls for an ecological sensibility."[155] "What process theology now seeks is a form of human-historical progress that simultaneously allows for the meeting of real human needs and for the renewed development of a rich and complex biosphere. It therefore opposes, first, that form of 'progress' which continues to destroy wholesale other living things."[156]

This theology conveys profound hope by asserting that God preserves the meaningfulness of our lives. "The image under which this operative growth of God's nature is best conceived, is that of a tender care that nothing be lost."[157] "The immediate

152. Cobb and Griffin, *Process Theology*, 8–9.

153. Cobb and Griffin, *Process Theology*, 100–101.

154. Cobb and Griffin, *Process Theology*, 126–27.

155. Cobb and Griffin, *Process Theology*, 153.

156. Cobb and Griffin, *Process Theology*, 149.

157. Whitehead, *Process and Reality*, 525; quoted in Cobb and Griffin,

facts of present action pass into permanent significance for the Universe."[158] This vaguely expressed hope finds more concrete affirmation in Personalism: "If values are conserved in this universe, they must be conserved as actual spiritual experiences of actually existing persons. Spirit is thus the highest aspect and function of personality, a token of its right to survive bodily death and develop forever."[159] "The conservation of value is the fundamental axiom of religion."[160]

Process Theology tends to put a strong emphasis on interfaith understanding. I find Process Theology to blend helpfully with Teilhardian theology. The strong Christology and the confident ruling principles of Teilhard can benefit from Process Theology's idea that God is affected by us and suffers with us, and uses only persuasion and not dictatorial power, thus preserving human freedom. Teilhard utters the great principle of progress: the universe evolving toward Christ, who is the Alpha and Omega. Whitehead's exaltation of the civilizational values of Truth, Beauty, Adventure, Art, and Peace provides a compass for progress. Personalism completes both of these philosophies by affirming the conservation of values and of persons.

EVOLUTION'S PURPOSE

What is further needed for the completion of a useful kind of Process Theology is the notion that evolution has a purpose. Teilhard thought that it did, and we can supplement him with more recent exploration of this idea. Steve McIntosh has written a fascinating book arguing that the supreme value triad of beauty, truth, and goodness has an effect on evolution, and he quotes David Griffin in support: "We are attracted to beauty, truth, and goodness because these values are entertained appetitively by the eros of

Process Theology, 122.

158. Whitehead, "Immortality," 698; quoted in Cobb and Griffin, *Process Theology*, 123.

159. Brightman, *Spiritual Life*, 48.

160. Höffding, *Philosophy*, 12.

the universe, whose appetites we feel."[161] McIntosh argues, "I have come to see that beauty, truth, and goodness are actually woven into the fabric of being. In other words, the aesthetic, the rational, and the moral, constitute essential irreducible dimensions of human experience."[162] All of these primary values have an objective pole and a subjective pole, and the subjective end is constantly evolving. Our understanding of goodness is always evolving.[163] McIntosh grieves the fact that postmodernists sometimes look at the subjective element of values and conclude that values are purely invented. This is short-sighted. Such relativism is destructive of insight. Those who recognize that "no value system is final or absolute can fall into a kind of value paralysis, becoming blind to comparative excellence."[164]

John Haught is a religious philosopher who addresses this issue. He writes that "purpose quite simply means the realizing of a value . . . Whitehead speaks about . . . the fundamental aim or purpose of the universe . . . simply to bring about more and more intense versions of *beauty* and the capacity to enjoy it . . . What Whitehead means by beauty is the synthesis of novelty on the one hand with order on the other. Beauty is the combining of contrast with harmony."[165]

Haught is building on Process Theology when he says, "A processive universe, by definition, is made up not of material bits but of transient events."[166] And these events are saved by God. God "saves the world as it passes into the immediacy of his own life."[167]

161. Griffin, *Religion and Scientific Naturalism*, 294; he is summarizing ideas from Whitehead's *Adventures of Ideas*; quoted in McIntosh, *Evolution's Purpose*, 68.

162. McIntosh, *Evolution's Purpose*, 84.

163. McIntosh, *Evolution's Purpose*, 87.

164. McIntosh, *Evolution's Purpose*, 102.

165. Haught, *John Haught Reader*, 253–54, relying on Whitehead, *Adventures of Ideas*, 252–96.

166. Haught, *John Haught Reader*, 300; original source is *Christianity and Science*, 153–65.

167. Whitehead, *Process and Reality*, 525; quoted in Haught, *John Haught Reader*, 292.

"Everything worthwhile that happens is received into God's own unfading experience, endowed with a permanent significance."[168] God "garners" everything of value. "Every event in the story of life and the universe is saved and transformed in the heart of God. In the drama of our universe, there is no absolute loss, and death does not have the final word."[169] This transformed result, this garnering of human experience, seems to correspond to Soloviev's concept of Sophia, "which contains within itself and unites with itself all particular living entities, or souls."[170]

In order to make sense of suffering and imperfection, Haught suggests that we reject the ancient idea of an original perfect design that was disturbed by sin, and "shift from the metaphor of divine governance toward that of God as goal—in accordance with a metaphysics of the future."[171] He suggests we drop the idea of a static ideal order that has been damaged, and think instead of an unfinished universe that is moving toward greater life. The concept of an "idealized cosmic order . . . presupposes a metaphysics in which change means the defilement of an initial integrity," which leads to theologies of expiation, "of reparation by paying a penalty in pain."[172] There are better ways of understanding Christ's work, ones that emphasize creation, recapitulation, and divinization.[173] With the expiation formula, "virtue, along with suffering, then has the meaning of repairing a lost perfection—instead of contributing to the growth of the world or the emergence of something truly new."[174] Haught uses Teilhard to strengthen his point that we need to have a dynamic worldview that recognizes we live in a developing universe, rather than one where a perfect past has been

168. Haught, *John Haught Reader*, 299; original source is *Christianity and Science*, 153–65.

169. Haught, *Cosmic Vision of Teilhard*, 142.

170. Soloviev ("Solovyov"), *Lectures*, 131.

171. Haught, *John Haught Reader*, 276; original source is *Resting on the Future*, 85–100.

172. Haught, *John Haught Reader*, 276.

173. Haught, *John Haught Reader*, 277.

174. Haught, *John Haught Reader*, 277.

damaged by human sin. The latter worldview would require us to find a "culprit," someone to blame for sin.[175] Rather, imperfection and free will are realities of this world, which make suffering and tragedy ever-present possibilities.

As opposed to either materialist or static idealistic philosophies, Haught advocates "anticipation, a third way of reading the universe . . . Aware that the cosmic story is far from over, it looks patiently and expectantly ahead for a possible meaning to it all . . . Something significant is working itself out in the universe."[176] "The 'purpose' of the universe, in this reading, is that of awakening—especially by way of life, mind, and religion—to rightness. And the purpose of our own personal lives is to augment this awakening."[177] Personal progress occurs under God's guidance. "The Lord will fulfill his purpose for me" (Ps 138:8) is an insight into Personality destiny. "The meek . . . will inherit the earth" (Matt 5:5) is a prophecy of planetary destiny.

McIntosh vigorously affirms purpose in the universe. He says: "The intrinsic purpose of evolution is growth toward goodness, beauty, and truth . . . The overall purpose of evolution is to increasingly grow toward perfection—to move toward ever-greater realizations of the beautiful, the true, and the good."[178] God could create a perfect world at any time, but that is not what *this* world is for. This world is meant to be an exercise in *achieved* perfection. That is the purpose of human evolution.

The human race has a spiritual destiny, however long it may take to achieve. I think that is what Isaiah was talking about when he wrote "the earth will be full of the knowledge of the Lord as the waters cover the sea" (Isa 11:9). A world where everyone really *knew God* would be a profoundly transformed world.

---

175. Haught, *Cosmic Vision of Teilhard*, 94, where he quotes Teilhard, *Christianity and Evolution*, 83–84.

176. Haught, *New Cosmic Story*, 35.

177. Haught, *New Cosmic Story*, 132.

178. McIntosh, *Evolution's Purpose*, 161.

In the meantime, suffering goes with the territory of "an *unfinished creation.*"[179] Suffering is not a punishment, but is inherent in the nature of an imperfect and unfinished universe. Especially in social life, there will be suffering in an imperfect world. As Ward writes, "God is creating a world in which tragedy is always threatening and often present. For it is a world spun from chaos and composed of a multiplicity of creatively free agents who shape the future at least partially through their own choices."[180] Suffering is gradually mitigated when progress is made, as people make spiritual progress and as societies pass through stages of development.

McIntosh writes of cultures moving through worldviews, from pre-traditional to traditional (religious) to modernist to postmodernist to evolutionary, the newest stage. "But unlike older worldviews, this evolutionary perspective also recognizes that every previous worldview contains important values that are necessary for the ongoing functionality of society."[181] One of the problems with the postmodern worldview, McIntosh says, is its tendency to trash the values of the previous stages. This tends to make traditionalists defensive, and cuts off helpful dialogue. One needs, rather, a deep appreciation of the values of previous worldviews. Cultural progress from stage to stage goes best when each stage "relies not only on the success of its previous stage; each new stage of cultural emergence also requires a degree of discontent" with the previous stage's "pathologies."[182]

Each stage needs to be a distinct advance upon the previous stage. "If a given stage remains 'too close' to its previous stage," it can fail. The example McIntosh gives is that many Islamic cultures in their traditional phase "are intermixed with too many pre-traditional values," such as "tribalism" and "virulent militancy."[183] Nor is Islam the only religion that is guilty of militancy and persecution of minority religions. Even Burmese Buddhism and Russian

179. Haught, *Cosmic Vision of Teilhard*, 153.

180. Ward, *Sharing*, 223, in Icecream e-book reader, chapter 6.

181. McIntosh, *Evolution's Purpose*, 199.

182. McIntosh, *Evolution's Purpose*, 208.

183. McIntosh, *Evolution's Purpose*, 209.

Orthodox Christianity have persecuted minority religions (my observation, not McIntosh's).

To understand where cultures are today it is necessary to understand the stages of progress through which cultures pass. McIntosh writes: "We can see from the historical record how the evolutionary emergence of democracy, prosperity, and worldcentric morality depends on relatively healthy forms of underlying traditional culture to provide a foundation of responsible values. And this tells us that where traditional cultures remain stagnant or unhealthy, some kind of 'reformation' will be needed before we can expect an 'enlightenment.'"[184]

Historical religions need reformations that redirect them to spiritual sources and that reject hypocrisy, greed, and superficiality. They also need enlightenments that open people's minds to the scientific level, and that allow for the emergence of intellectual freedom. An enlightenment in culture tends to suggest that we must find ways of balancing spiritual and scientific thinking. One of the fundamental roles of philosophy is to perform this balancing. The true goal of philosophy is to attain a unified worldview that allows for both spiritual truth and scientific fact. Philosophy is very personal, since it is the individual who must seek a balanced view for him- or herself.

Some religious people resist a scientific worldview; others see no conflict with science, and seek to allow religion and science to coexist. Science does not require materialism or scientism, the belief that only science can explain things, and that everything is determined by material causes. Scientism is just a new wrinkle on the old materialism. Many scientists fall into the trap of materialistic scientism, which reduces mind to an accidental by-product of purely material causation. However, "if the ultimate explanation of mind is a primordial cosmic state of mindlessness, then why do scientists still trust that their own minds can lead us to right understanding or truth?"[185]

---

184. McIntosh, *Evolution's Purpose*, 209–10.
185. Haught, *Cosmic Vision of Teilhard*, 163.

In order to examine the "worldcentric" views for which Mc-Intosh calls, it is necessary to look into the hope for interreligious understanding and peace.

4

Unity among All Religions
Truth in Diverse Religions

The traditional scheme for considering available attitudes toward religions other than one's own has been that there are
three choices: exclusivism, inclusivism, and pluralism. Exclusivism
claims that the truth about salvation is confined to one religion or
one sect of religion.[1] Exclusivism can manifest intense hostility
toward "other" religions or other versions of the supposedly true
religion. An interesting story in this regard is from editor Mickey
Maudlin: "As a young evangelical, I was socialized to see the biggest threat to the church as theological liberalism. But now I think
the biggest threat is Christian tribalism, where God's interests are
reduced to and measured by those sharing your history, tradition,
and beliefs, and where one needs an 'enemy' in order for you to
feel 'right with God.'"[2] The inclusivist and pluralist options reject
such toxic exclusivism.

Inclusivism allows that "the salvific process" can take place
in other religions, but that it is still Christ who really saves. Some

---

1. Hick, *Christian Theology of Religions*, 19.
2. Maudlin, "Rob Bell's Hell."

versions of Christian inclusivism hold that Jews, Hindus, and Muslims may be saved by Christ, even if they are "unaware of it."[3]

John Hick took a pluralist position, arguing that the generosity that inclusivists intend is more logically promoted by a pluralist viewpoint: "The ultimate ineffable Reality is capable of being authentically experienced in terms of different sets of human concepts, *as* Yahweh, *as* the Holy Trinity, *as* Allah, *as* Shiva."[4] He found a similarity in all the faiths: "These traditions involve different human conceptions of the Real."[5]

Before delving deeper into pluralist philosophy (and an important critique of it), I want to explore some inclusivist viewpoints.

OTHER SCRIPTURES

I will consider two theologians whom I would consider inclusivist, although they do not apply that term to themselves, namely Jacques Dupuis and Karl Rahner. Let us begin with a vital spiritual question.

Was the Spirit somehow active in the composition of the various Scriptures of world religions? Some important Christian thinkers have said yes. The Catholic document *Redemptoris Missio* said, "It is the Spirit who sows the 'seeds of the Word' present in various customs and cultures, preparing them for full maturity in Christ"; this picks up on the terminology used by Justin Martyr, who wrote of the Logos *spermatikos*.[6] Jacques Dupuis affirms, "God, to whom alone belongs the initiative of any divine-human encounter, has willed to speak to the nations themselves, through the religious experience of their prophets."[7] The emphasis here is on experience: "All religious experience becomes truly personal in the Spirit. In the order of divine-human relationships, the Spirit, in

---

3. Hick, *Christian Theology of Religions*, 19–20.

4. Hick, *Christian Theology of Religions*, 25.

5. Hick, *Christian Theology of Religions*, 27.

6. *Redemptoris Missio* (RM) 28; Dupuis, *Toward Religious Pluralism*, 243.

7. Dupuis, *Toward Religious Pluralism*, 247.

the last analysis, is God rendered personally present to the human being—God felt by the human being in the depths of the human heart."[8] He also affirms that there is a three-stage hierarchy, from revelations "to the hearts of seers" of all nations, to the revelation to Israel, to the revelation through Jesus Christ.[9] This is not to assert that the New Testament is the full and perfect revelation. "The fullness of revelation is not, properly speaking, the written word of the New Testament"; the full revelation is "the very person of Jesus Christ, his deeds and his words, his life, his death, and his resurrection"; the New Testament is the "interpretation, the authentic memorial, of that revelation."[10]

Dupuis affirms the view of Pope John Paul II, who wrote, "Every authentic prayer is under the influence of the Spirit 'who intercedes insistently for us ... because we do not even know how to pray as we ought' [Rom 8:26] ... Every authentic prayer is called forth by the Holy Spirit, who is mysteriously present in the heart of every person."[11] Dupuis says "God has uttered initial words to human beings through the prophets of the nations—a word whose traces can be found in the sacred scriptures of the world's religious traditions"; however, in Jesus Christ, "God utters his decisive word in him who is 'the Word.'"[12] God is revealing Godself through numerous Scriptures; but the definitive and "decisive" revelation is in the person of Jesus Christ. The word of God has never stopped acting upon humanity, in every culture. Dupuis repeatedly quotes John 1:9: "The Word was the true light that enlightens every human being coming into the world."[13] Other religions "too can be made

---

8. Dupuis, *Toward Religious Pluralism*, 244.

9. Dupuis, *Toward Religious Pluralism*, 250.

10. Dupuis, *Toward Religious Pluralism*, 248.

11. Dupuis, *Toward Religious Pluralism*, 175. He is quoting John Paul II's statement at the World Day of Prayer for Peace, published by Commission Pontificale "Justitia et Pax." It is published in *Bulletin* (Secretariat for Non-Christians) 64/22/1 (1987).

12. Dupuis, *Toward Religious Pluralism*, 250.

13. Dupuis, *Toward Religious Pluralism*, 319; see 288, 294.

use of by God as channels of his salvation."[14] This parallels natural theology, the notion that moral and spiritual instincts pervade the whole universe and every individual mind. This echoes the Stoic concept of Logos, and also certain biblical passages. Paul said, regarding Gentiles, "What can be known about God is plain to them, because God has shown it to them . . . what the law requires is written on their hearts" (Rom 1:19; 2:15). There is a divine spark within every person that serves to stimulate spiritual desire. The spark may not provide very much in the way of specific and detailed teaching, thus the enormous differences in religions. But it does provide a kind of spiritual intuition, seeking to impart a basic spiritual reason: "Truly it is the spirit in a mortal, the breath of the Almighty, that makes for understanding" (Job 32:8).

Karl Rahner made the classic statement about honest believers of other religions being "anonymous Christians." He writes: "There can be no doubt that someone who has no concrete, historical contact with the explicit preaching of Christianity can nevertheless be a justified person who lives by the grace of Christ . . . [W]e can speak of 'anonymous Christians.'"[15] Stated otherwise, "It is *a priori* quite possible to suppose that there are supernatural, grace-filled elements in non-Christian religions."[16]

I would concur with Dupuis that religions are not all equally valid (as is implied by Hick), but that the Spirit does speak to the other religions and cultures, even though these revelations are shaped by the mentality and existing beliefs of the people receiving the revelation, and so are not philosophically congruent with the revelations to Israel or through Jesus. In fact, I would add, even the revelations to Israel and to the Christian church are full of adaptation and even distortion by the humans receiving them. Everything that is touched by humans is formed and interpreted by humans. All revelation is adapted and shaped by human minds. There is no crystal-clear and uninterpreted message from God. "The spirits of prophets are subject to the prophets" (1 Cor 14:32).

14. Dupuis, *Toward Religious Pluralism*, 306.

15. Rahner, *Foundations of Christian Faith*, 176.

16. Rahner, "Christianity and the Non-Christian Religions," 215.

Dupuis opines that there is "a Trinitarian structure, no matter how inchoate and imperfect, in all human experience of the Divine."[17] Raimon Panikkar sees a parallel between Brahman, Ishvara, and Atman; and Father, Son, and Spirit.[18] John Cobb argues that a "mutual transformation will result from the osmosis between the complementary approaches . . . between the worldviews" of Christianity and Buddhism.[19]

The logic of Dupuis's reasoning would seem to indicate that these religions are potentially evolving toward a greater recognition of Trinitarian patterns, and thus towards an openness to Christian theology, but he never says that. I think he resists that because it is suggestive of "fulfillment theory, according to which Christian truth 'brings to completion'—in a one-sided process—the fragmentary truths it finds sown outside"; there should, instead, be "mutual enrichment and transformation."[20] God seems to intend that people find different paths to salvation through their inherited religions. I would say that these others are drawing upon the Spirit and upon the Word, and so are drawing on the Creator power of Jesus, though unawares. A similar view is this: "If people, moved by the Spirit of God, exercise faith in God, no matter what revelation of God they have, they are saved by the merits of Christ."[21]

The papal document *Dialogue and Proclamation* argues, "'in the sincere practice of what is good in their own religious traditions' that they respond positively to God's offer of grace (29)."[22] This document does not see interreligious dialogue as a route to

---

17. Dupuis, *Toward Religious Pluralism*, 276.

18. Panikkar, *Unknown Christ of Hinduism*; cited by Dupuis, *Toward Religious Pluralism*, 266.

19. Dupuis, *Toward Religious Pluralism*, 382, summarizing Cobb and Ives, *Emptying God*.

20. Dupuis, *Toward Religious Pluralism*, 326.

21. Sanders, "Inclusivism," 48.

22. Dupuis, *Toward Religious Pluralism*, 366.

converting the other. Rather, "the aim of interreligious dialogue is 'a deeper conversion of all towards God.'"[23]

None of this means that the dialogue participants should engage in "toning down of deep convictions."[24] Nor does a "soteriocentric" or "theocentric" viewpoint require the tamping down of "Christocentric" views.[25] "That God spoke 'in many and various ways' before speaking through his Son (Heb 1:1) is not incidental; nor is" it just a thing of the past.[26] "The decisiveness of the Son's advent in the flesh in Jesus Christ does not cancel the universal presence and action of the Word and the Spirit," in other religions.[27] The truth of Christian revelation neither excludes nor includes "all other truth"; rather, it is *related* to, and *complementary* to, the truth in other religions.[28] Dupuis supports Teilhard's vision of an eventual convergence of world religions in the "universal Christ."[29] Of course, he leaves many questions unanswered: Will these other religions come to affirm Jesus *by name*, or the biblical God *as such*? I think, for Teilhard, the answer is "yes," but Dupuis is unclear about his answer. His resistance to fulfillment theory might have suggested a "no" answer. But then, he *does* quote Teilhard about a "'marvelous convergence,' to take place in the eschaton, of all things and all religious traditions in the Reign of God and in the Christ-omega."[30] Ultimately, this does represent a form of inclusivism and of fulfillment theory, I think, but with an insistence on showing respect for the other religions, and on emphasizing complementarity and dialogue. Dupuis does not want to identify as an inclusivist because he thinks that term denotes arrogance, which he finds repulsive. Mark Heim has shown that inclusivism can be

23. Dupuis, *Toward Religious Pluralism*, 367.

24. Dupuis, *Toward Religious Pluralism*, 379.

25. Dupuis, *Toward Religious Pluralism*, 377, 373.

26. Dupuis, *Toward Religious Pluralism*, 387.

27. Dupuis, *Toward Religious Pluralism*, 387.

28. Dupuis, *Toward Religious Pluralism*, 388–89.

29. Dupuis, *Toward Religious Pluralism*, 390. He is quoting Teilhard, *Christianity and Evolution*, 130.

30. Dupuis, *Toward Religious Pluralism*, 389–90.

very respectful and interested in the details of other religions.[31] I examine Heim's position towards the end of the next section.

ENGAGED DIALOGUE BETWEEN RELIGIONS

Paul Knitter identifies himself as a pluralist, or someone who favors correlational dialogue with other religions, open to the possibility that "Buddha may have as 'saving' a word to speak as does Christ."[32] Knitter wants us to think of "Jesus as delivering God's *decisive but not total* word."[33] Therefore, "In a qualified but still real sense, persons of other religious paths are 'unfulfilled' without Christ. . . . Christians . . . must be as deeply open to being enlightened, fulfilled, and transformed by the Word spoken and embodied for them in persons of other religious paths."[34]

Knitter says that real loyalty to Jesus has more to do with *doing* than with *believing*. "Fidelity to the New Testament confessions about Jesus is essentially and primarily a matter of acting with and like Jesus, not of insisting that he is above all others."[35] "Christians would . . . diagnose the cause of suffering as having to do with the way *people* treat each other; and that means with practices and systems of *injustice*. If there are slaves, one must address the pharaoh. If the temple has become a den of thieves, one must confront the chief priests and elders."[36]

As for openness to other religions, "Christ is the way that is open to other ways."[37] Many Christians are coming to realize that the goal of those who are loyal to Jesus should be to spread the kingdom of God, and only secondarily the church. "There has been a momentous shift in Christian, especially Roman Catholic, understanding of what the church is all about, a shift from an

31. Heim, *Salvations*, 141–49, 170–71.

32. Knitter, *Jesus and the Other Names*, 47.

33. Knitter, *Jesus and the Other Names*, 78.

34. Knitter, *Jesus and the Other Names*, 79.

35. Knitter, *Jesus and the Other Names*, 69.

36. Knitter, *Jesus and the Other Names*, 99.

37. Knitter, *Jesus and the Other Names*, 107.

ecclesiocentric . . . to what the Roman Catholic bishops of Asia call a 'regnocentric' or Kingdom-centered perspective."[38] This continues and expands upon how a document of "Vatican II, *Gaudium et Spes*, puts it: 'The Church has but one sole purpose—that the Kingdom of God may come and salvation of the human race may be accomplished.'"[39] The key Vatican documents that expressed this view were *Redemptoris Missio* (RM, 1989) and *Dialogue and Proclamation* (DP, 1991), which saw other religions as authentic approaches to God. "In a Kingdom-centered orientation of the church and mission, other religions are not only 'ways of salvation,' they are, more precisely and more engagingly, 'ways of the Kingdom' (*viae Regni*)."[40] The church needs to serve the kingdom. "The one larger reality of the Kingdom *cannot* be encompassed and contained within the church. . . . The church is meant to be a *servant* of the broader and more important reign of God."[41]

However, Pope John Paul II pushed back against this kingdom-centered idea, inserting language into both of these documents that reined in the regnocentric idea. He inserted language into RM: "In making 'man's earthly needs' the focus of mission, 'the Kingdom tends to become something completely human and secularized . . . *The Kingdom cannot be detached either from the Christ or from the Church*. . . . If the Kingdom is separated from Jesus, it is no longer the Kingdom of God which he revealed. . . . Christ is the one savior of all, the *only one able to reveal God and lead to God*.'"[42] Thus the two documents have passages which speak both for and against a new kingdom-centered concept of mission. Knitter shares the pope's resistance to any "'reduction' of mission praxis to purely social or political or economic concerns."[43] He wants the human works to be "also spiritual works," and argues that "to place work for the this-worldly realization of the Kingdom *first* does not

38. Knitter, *Jesus and the Other Names*, 108.
39. Knitter, *Jesus and the Other Names*, 109.
40. Knitter, *Jesus and the Other Names*, 118.
41. Knitter, *Jesus and the Other Names*, 126.
42. Knitter, *Jesus and the Other Names*, 127–28, 133.
43. Knitter, *Jesus and the Other Names*, 130.

mean to place concern for the Spirit *second*."⁴⁴ Knitter feels that the pope's traditional Christology is fatal to a regnocentric view. "With such an understanding of Jesus, the universality of the Kingdom is continually reduced to the particularity of the church."⁴⁵ And yet, both documents left in place some groundbreaking language about deep dialogue with other religions as a *necessary*, not just allowable, part of mission. Christianity may need to be corrected and changed, as a result of such dialogue.⁴⁶ Knitter desires the situation where "missionaries go forth both to teach *and be taught*, that both activities are essential and integral parts of the missionary's job."⁴⁷ "To hold up Christian tradition as the sole source or norm for theology is to disrespect what God has revealed elsewhere. The Christian Word is *incomplete* without other Words."⁴⁸

I find myself wanting to take a middle position between Knitter and Pope John Paul II. In mission, dialogue, and the role of the church I lean toward Knitter. In Christology, I support the pope's emphasis on the uniqueness of Jesus. I do agree with Knitter that the pope tended to make an absolute out of the church. So I ask: Is there a way to affirm the unique divinity of Jesus without making a fetish of the church? Is there a way to have a strong Christology and also a strong dialogue with other religions? I think there is.

I think what will really speak to people of other religions is not Christian doctrine or theology, so much as the character of Jesus, the most compelling and interesting person in human history. The Gospels *have* made a deep appeal to people of other religions, from Jalaluddin Rumi to Mahatma Gandhi to Martin Buber.

Knitter hopes for "a *representational Christology* that holds up Jesus as a decisive representation or embodiment or revelation of God's saving love—a love that 'pre-dates' Jesus"; he rejects the idea that "Without Jesus such love would not be active in the world"

---

44. Knitter, *Jesus and the Other Names*, 131.
45. Knitter, *Jesus and the Other Names*, 135.
46. Knitter, *Jesus and the Other Names*, 139–40.
47. Knitter, *Jesus and the Other Names*, 145.
48. Knitter, *Jesus and the Other Names*, 158.

and that "salvation can *only* come from Jesus Christ."[49] I want to take a middle position between these two Christologies. I say that God's saving love did predate the earth life of Jesus, but it did not predate Jesus in his heavenly self, since he created this very world. A Creator Christology can prevent falling into either a weak "representational" Christology or a rigid fundamentalist Christology.

Sometimes the monotheists find allies in unexpected places. A recent book that calls itself "an interfaith primer" contains an assertion by its Hindu author: "Hinduism teaches the oneness of God . . . While Hindu tradition affirms the oneness of God, it is radically pluralistic in the sense that it teaches that the names by which the one God may be called are literally limitless. . . . Ultimately, for Hindus, no single name can define, contain, or limit the limitless."[50] While it is doubtful that the average Hindu in the street thinks this way, this Hindu intellectual could be called a monotheist.

What about possible agreement on fundamental values? This seems to be one of the partly articulated assumptions of Knitter: that there will be agreement about respect for women, dignity for the poor, and justice for the marginalized. "Knitter argues that all religions are to be judged as to their truthfulness in so far as they promote the process of liberation, a process which Christians call 'the kingdom.'"[51] Thus, D'Costa argues, "Knitter's alleged pluralism is in fact working with very specific and exclusive truth claims," that different religions show quite different levels of conformity with these truth claims, which "severely undermines the possibility of using these criteria to establish that all religions have an equal claim to truth."[52] If Knitter's truth criteria were to be spelled out more fully, they would be seen to be quite Western and modern in nature, and not to be found in equal degree in the Eastern religions. D'Costa argues that pluralists are, in fact, exclusivists. What D'Costa has established for me is that a liberationist value-scale

49. Knitter, *Jesus and the Other Names*, 133.
50. Rambachan, "To Recognize and Love God," 3–4.
51. D'Costa, "Impossibility of a Pluralist View of Religions," 230.
52. D'Costa, "Impossibility of a Pluralist View of Religions," 230.

will not discover an equality between religions, and that pluralists usually do not spell out their truth claims clearly.

I think Creator Christology holds the key to solving some of the dilemmas in the theological debate about pluralism. Is Jesus the one way to approach God, or do many paths lead to God? Yes (to both). The many paths, if they are spiritually progressive, eventually lead people to Jesus, either here or in the afterlife. The Spirit that is active in the human race eventually draws people to the one who is the gate (John 10:9). First Peter speaks of Jesus preaching "to the spirits in prison" (3:19), and one does not preach to beings who are incapable of responding or converting. "The gospel was proclaimed even to the dead, so that . . . they might live in the spirit as God does" (1 Pet 4:6). The preaching had a saving purpose. And again, "the hour is coming, and is now here, when the dead will hear the voice of the Son of God, and those who hear will live" (John 5:25). This may be part of what Paul was driving at when he wrote: "At the name of Jesus every knee should bend, in heaven and on earth and under the earth" (Phil 2:10). The "divine perseverance . . . pursu[es] us to the end."[53]

We should reject the idea of God being vindictive. Even the author of Lamentations saw this: "he does not willingly afflict or grieve anyone" (Lam 3:33). And again, "I have no pleasure in the death of anyone, says the Lord God" (Ezek 18:32). Why would God's forgiveness and love not extend beyond the grave? What good is it to keep anyone in a hell forever, where there is no possibility of repair or repentance?

Mark Heim wishes for dialogue between religions, but strongly questions the pluralist philosophy of academic theologians like John Hick and Paul Knitter. John Hick said that all the faiths have a similar goal: "Salvation/liberation . . . is the central concern of all the great world religions. . . . [S]alvation, in this sense of an actual change in human beings from natural self-centredness towards a recentring in the Divine, the Ultimate, the Real."[54] The "Real" becomes the name for "God" or "the Absolute," for Hick.

53. Fackre, "Divine Perseverance," 73.
54. Hick, *Christian Theology of Religions*, 18.

Heim looks at Hick's thesis and disagrees with two of its founding assumptions: "that the realm of ultimate reality consists of a single, noumenal element which Hick calls 'the Real,'" and that they all seek the same kind of salvation, that "one identical salvific process is taking place in them all."[55] When Hick talks about religions, he seems to say that their particular beliefs, their "mythologies," do not matter. All are roughly equal since each is an attempt to approach "the Real." Hick decided that "the Incarnation should be understood as a symbolic or metaphorical or mythic rather than as a literal truth."[56] Heim paraphrases Hick's position thus: "The difference seems to be that religious believers differ over matters whose truth or falsity makes no difference to true religion."[57] This kind of pluralism is really a put-down of all religious beliefs.

Heim finds Knitter's approach just as problematic. Knitter also avoids discussing particular beliefs, putting the emphasis instead upon social activism. As long as they have some social *praxis* that contributes to justice, they are all seeking salvation, and so we should take a "soteriocentric" approach. Heim says Knitter is simply creating a new kind of religious norm, while ignoring the religions' own norms. "In insisting on a *praxis* and justice norm, are soteriocentrists not simply arguing for one kind of religious norm above others?"[58] Soteriocentric pluralism "is untenable . . . The liberation theology of religions claims an absolute validity for the praxis of justice and liberation. The argument that particularistic religious claims lead inevitably to domination, while claims to know what justice requires lead to liberation is incoherent."[59]

Looking at the main pluralistic approaches, Heim sees them as making secular, academic assumptions. Pluralism assumes, "Only as demythologized, adapted to the categories of critical historical thought, put in the context of Western understandings of epistemology, and measured against modern conceptions of

---

55. Heim, *Salvations*, 23, 26.

56. Hick, *Problems of Religious Pluralism*, 11.

57. Heim, *Salvations*, 31.

58. Heim, *Salvations*, 94.

59. Heim, *Salvations*, 97.

equality and justice can these religions be pronounced valid."[60] Especially does Knitter's approach represent a "movement toward the authority of social scientific categories."[61] The religions' "rationale must be given in terms that supersede the religions themselves."[62]

A similar point is made by Douglas Harink. "Those who thus seek to rescue the religions from ethnocentrism, parochialism, and exclusivism, themselves simply instantiate just one more such vision (that of liberal intellectual elites who have achieved the 'global gaze') and propose it as the universal truth."[63]

Heim prefers an approach of "orientational pluralism," in which people all speak from their own orientations, which are legitimately different; "they make some claim to the universal value of their affirmations," and yet "they teach some measure of humility about our capacity to understand reality in its fullness."[64] One is not forced to make the implausible claim that all religions are seeking the same Reality and have the same goals. Heim, then, ends up affirming that inclusivism is a natural and expected viewpoint.[65] He wants an inclusivism that retains humility and a desire to truly understand the other.

An interesting take that need not be labeled "pluralist," but can certainly be labeled "open-minded," is that taken by Bob Robinson. He argues that "exemplary Christology" can make for fruitful "interreligious encounters."[66] The phrase "exemplary Christology" refers to following Christ's own example, his own encounters with Gentiles and Samaritans as paradigmatic for encounters *we* may have with non-Christians. He rejects the idea that Christology goes against such encounters. Rather, look to what Jesus did when he encountered Syro-Phoenicians, Romans, and Samaritans, and what he said about them. There are "elements in [Jesus'] teaching

60. Heim, *Salvations*, 109.

61. Heim, *Salvations*, 203.

62. Heim, *Salvations*, 218.

63. Harink, *Paul among the Postliberals*, 246.

64. Heim, *Salvations*, 143–44.

65. Heim, *Salvations*, 152.

66. Robinson, *Jesus and the Religions*, 10.

and actions that respond positively to these 'outsiders,'" namely, Gentiles and Samaritans.[67] In his introductory sermon in Luke 4, Jesus goes out of his way to show how God ministered to Gentiles in some scriptural stories. First he announces the beginning of his mission by reading the stunning prophecy from Isaiah 61, adding a clause from Isaiah 35: "The Spirit of the Lord is upon me . . . He has sent me to proclaim release to the captives and recovery of sight to the blind, to let the oppressed go free . . . Today this scripture has been fulfilled in your hearing" (Luke 4:18, 21). But he senses the grumbling of the crowd, and their desire to see wonders, so he continues: "The truth is, there were many widows in Israel in the time of Elijah, when the heaven was shut up for three years and six months, and there was a severe famine over all the land; yet Elijah was sent to none of them except to a widow at Zarephath in Sidon. There were also many lepers in Israel in the time of the prophet Elisha, and none of them was cleansed except Naaman the Syrian" (Luke 4:25–27). The Nazareth crowd becomes enraged when Jesus points out how Elijah and Elishah were sent to heal only Gentiles. In Jesus' telling, "the salvation of God is open to a range of outsiders, while insiders are left out."[68] The Nazarenes' national pride gets in the way of their really hearing the message of Jesus.

This and other stories are a rebuke against Israel for its "nationalist insularity." Robinson continues: "The contemporary church might well consider the implications of such a rebuke for some of its own attitudes towards those of other faiths given that Jesus is seen in this passage (and others) to affirm at least some dimension of the faith of 'outsiders.'"[69] The way that Jesus uses Isaiah 61 is to affirm mercy and forgiveness. What follows, the Elijah-Elisha stories about healings for Gentiles, shows "that God's saving and healing presence is not confined to the ancient borders of Israel."[70]

---

67. Robinson, *Jesus and the Religions*, 25.
68. Robinson, *Jesus and the Religions*, 30.
69. Robinson, *Jesus and the Religions*, 27.
70. Robinson, *Jesus and the Religions*, 33.

An example of a spiritually engaged group that is both inter-faith and Christian is the Church of Conscious Harmony in Austin, Texas. "This is a community that understands and is receptive to the treasures that exist within each of the world's religions. Our deeply rooted faith in our own tradition enables us to welcome and receive other faiths without sacrificing our own or imposing ours on another."[71] If one is securely grounded in a religious tradition, that grounding will not be threatened by an open-minded exploration of other traditions. "Whoever is not against us is for us" (Mark 9:40).

An important forum for interfaith understanding that has been going on for over a hundred years is the Parliament of World's Religions. One participant writes, "The Parliament has changed my life and has listened. I feel that we have learned to listen to each other and acknowledge our differences."[72]

These approaches place an emphasis on respectful dialogue between religions, and not on a creedal agreement between religions on the concept of God or the transcendent.

SPIRITUAL UNITY

Spiritual unity between those of different faiths and beliefs is a necessary precursor to interreligious peace. Spiritual unity does not mean that we will all think alike or believe alike, but that we will all *strive* alike, that we honestly seek God's will. Spiritual unity arises from our ability to recognize honest spiritual motivation in others, even in those who have completely different belief systems. It involves letting consideration and respect be more important than being right or winning arguments.

Often the barrier against spiritual unity is not doctrinal so much as it is social. If a Christian is perceived as being close friends with Muslims or Hindus, his fellow Christians may question whether he is really a Christian any more. Anything that

---

71. Genung, "Finding Harmony," 25.
72. Bhagavati, "How the AIDS Pandemic Changed My Life," 64.

challenges or undermines people's religious identity can be seen as a threat. Such tribalistic positions remind me of the false witnesses against Jesus who said that he claimed he would destroy the Temple (Matt 26:61). These critics perceived him as a threat to the Temple and therefore to the community. There is always the danger that people will idolize the symbols of their faith, and defend these symbols to the death, even while betraying that for which the symbols are meant to stand.

Spiritual unity comes from the similarity of values instilled in the lives of all those who wholeheartedly seek spiritual guidance; and from the recognition that such value-motivation can be found among people whose beliefs differ. It is the individual's *experience* in religion that really matters, along with acceptance of the fact that only God has the last word in matters of spiritual truth.

Jesus did not advocate spiritual *sameness*; he called for tolerance and sympathetic spirituality among people who walk different paths, but whose paths converge in God. He shocked his apostles when he responded to their complaint about a strange preacher who "does not follow with us," by saying "Do not stop him; for whoever is not against you is for you" (Luke 9:49–50).

He was not concerned with social control, but with spiritual growth. Elsewhere he emphasized the saving value of a simple act of kindness: "Whoever gives even a cup of cold water to one of these little ones in the name of a disciple—truly I tell you, none of these will lose their reward" (Matthew 10:42). The sincerity of the act of kindness is recognized and honored by God. These sayings speak of an attitude of generosity and acceptance, not of dogmatic correctness or of social belonging, much less of exclusivity. Without any reference to beliefs or dogmas, Jesus pronounces someone saved on the basis of offering a cup of water. This shows that people *are* capable of doing good deeds, and that good deeds matter. "Whoever does good is from God" (3 John 11).

Spiritual unity is not a uniformity of belief; it is more like a synchronizing of spiritual motivation. None of us knows all of God, but each of us knows *something* of God: "truly it is the spirit in a mortal, the breath of the Almighty, that makes for understanding" (Job 32:8). Everyone has the breath of the Almighty within them.

Spiritual unity begins with individuals sincerely desiring to do the will of God (Mark 3:35; John 7:17). It also requires the ability to recognize this motivation in others. It affirms the validity of the individual's "walk with God" (Mic 6:8), recognizing that "these are the ones who, when they hear the word, hold it fast in an honest and good heart, and bear fruit with patient endurance" (Luke 8:15). If we can recognize that the Hindu or the Muslim can also have a "walk with God," and can also hold fast a word of truth "in an honest and good heart," then we are capable of reaching spiritual unity with such a person. The Scriptures of Sikhism say, "One who submits to the will of God attains Liberation."[73]

Of course, this is not just a hazy desire to "be nice." This is *religious* motivation, based on the consciousness of relatedness to God or the Way. True unity is inseparable from a life of faith in God and progress in insight. If there is no God, no source of true values, then values are mere inventions, and each value-inventor is an isolated soul in a universe of alienation. If spirit is an illusion and God a fiction, then all spiritual or social values are only a glorification of natural appetites and psychological projections. The political consequence of such a belief would be tyranny. Atheistic philosophy offers no real defense against totalitarianism.

Only religion can really affirm the value of both the individual and the whole. Voluntary identification with God is the only way to have both unity and freedom, to avoid the coerced "unity" (uniformity) imposed by tyranny. "Belief in objective value is necessary to the very idea of a rule which is not tyranny or an obedience which is not slavery."[74] Lewis uses the term "*Tao*" to refer to traditional religions' belief that there is a moral law in the universe. Those who craft new ideologies based on "reason" are really exploiting the *Tao* while dismembering it: "What purport to be new systems or (as they now call them) 'ideologies,' all consist

73. Nanak, *Japji Sahib* Pauri 15.
74. Lewis, *Abolition of Man*, 84–85.

of fragments from the *Tao* itself, arbitrarily wrenched from their context in the whole and then swollen to madness in their isolation, yet still owing to the *Tao* and to it alone such validity as they possess."[75] Humanist philosophies dismember biblical teachings, seize upon some of the fragments, and swell them up to a supreme position.

The belief that true value is based in God is what distinguishes religious from non-religious idealism. "The meaning of our existence is not invented by ourselves, but rather detected."[76] If there is a moral *Tao*, it is up to us to *detect* it.

If values are real, then, as we discover them we will move toward unity, without losing creativity. Our perceptions of values may differ, but they are the *same* values (on God's side), and so "everything that rises must converge"[77]—or at least *harmonize*. A unity of supreme loyalties does not obliterate human diversity but it does extinguish hatred and fear.

Each person must be allowed to experience a unique walk with God, yet each truth-motivated person will seek unity and peace with the rest of the planetary family.

Perhaps the most touching of Jesus' prayers (on record) is the plea "that they may all be one . . . I in them and you in me, that they may become completely one, so that the world may know that you have sent me and have loved them even as you have loved me" (John 17:21, 23). The mutual love among Christ-followers should be a testimony of God's love for everyone, and thus a means of drawing the whole world into one, spiritually. However, this will not work if religions are overly withdrawn and ritualistic, nor if they are overly committed to external social activism, which is inseparable from political ambition. Today Christianity is so woven into the social fabric of the West that it is hardly able to proclaim its spiritual ideals without reference to politics. We are social and so must religion be, but the ideals of Jesus start with the *person*, changing society by changing the individual. If religious philosophy fails to focus on

---

75. Lewis, *Abolition of Man*, 56.

76. Frankl, *Man's Search for Meaning*, 157.

77. Teilhard de Chardin, "Faith in Man," in *Future of Man*, 192.

Jesus' central message, it can only freeze up into creedalism, or else meander about without moorings, swept along by societal trends.

Spiritual unity must be founded upon an enlightened concept of personality: balancing the spiritual value of the individual with the all-encompassing unity of God, the Father/Mother of all persons, and the destiny of all who hunger for truth. Others may conceive of "God" differently: "Conceived of as having no name, it is the Originator of heaven and earth; conceived of as having a name, it is the Mother of all things."[78] Seeking to harmonize with the will of the Originator or Mother is the same fundamental motive as seeking to do the will of God.

This is not to say that God or the Originator will be conceived in the same way by Christianity and Taoism, but that there is a commonality of motivation that can be discovered and described, and which can form a basis for mutual understanding.

I have said that everyone has the breath of the Almighty within them. And I do think that God seeks to reach every human heart. This does not mean that all religions are equally valid, or that Christ is no more significant than Lao Tzu or Buddha. It simply means that every human being has equal freedom to seek out the truth, and each one's experience is precious, because it reflects the activity of God's spirit in that one's soul.

God seeks to draw us to truth and goodness through their persuasive power. The love of God is non-coercive: "It is inwardly that we must come together, and in entire freedom."[79] "God's creative activity is persuasive, not controlling."[80]

God surely values our creative originality too much to demand that we all become alike; and yet the Father of diversity is also the Source of unity. God is the ultimate goal of all the pure in heart.

78. Lao Tzu, *Tao te Ching* 1, translated by James Legge.

79. Teilhard de Chardin, "Some Reflections on Progress," in *Future of Man*, 74.

80. Cobb and Griffin, *Process Theology*, 57.

CHURCHES AND SOCIAL ACTIVISM

I need to introduce a cautionary note here. The church should not attempt to direct social processes, but should focus on the inner process of faith and insight as the key to fostering spiritual fellowship. The ideals of Jesus would then have their greatest social effect (directly upon the religious community, indirectly upon society at large).

The gospel positively affects society first by saving and transforming the individual; second by surprising others with the loving sociability of the saved, both amongst themselves and toward everyone; and third, by slowly penetrating secular society through the activity of changed individuals in secular affairs. But this third step must remain an unconscious one insofar as the religious *group* is concerned. This is another possible meaning of "do not let your left hand know what your right hand is doing" (Matt 6:3). Religious groups should not make secular influence a group goal. For if spiritual goals start to be absorbed by political goals, religion becomes merely the servant of some social trend. This can be a sneaky devil, for it includes not only a church's espousal of political causes, or an individual's unwise identification of Jesus with a political platform, but also careerism and the infighting of church politics.

Churches sometimes espouse all too much social idealism. They may have a healthy interest in their neighbors, but for that very reason it is necessary to have a well thought out philosophy of the separation of powers so that religious groups are not as politicized and divided as they are now. Infatuation with social causes or support for national states makes religious groups indistinguishable from political ones. Conservative religion has usually been politicized by supporting the status quo, by yearning to return to an imagined past, and by virtue of their accumulation of wealth. Its sometime vehement renunciation of "the world" is surpassed only by its own worldliness. "Liberation theologies" rebel against this kind of religion by becoming even more frankly political and partisan.

It is true that Jesus brought spiritual pressure to bear upon such social problems as racial and class hatred, religious conceit, fraud, and oppression. But this does not make him a political activist, as his message speaks not of social structures, but of personal attitudes. He proposed no political solutions to social problems, but, by bringing love into the lives of rich and poor, learned and laborer, Jew and Greek, he provided the leaven that can work its way throughout society and transform people on both sides of every social issue—and that is spiritual pressure. He used none of the methods of political pressure, but focused on a religious fellowship that would be exclusively devoted to spiritual regeneration. A church that takes up political tasks with even the best desire for social justice will end up with an investment in material structures and a consequent distortion of spiritual goals. Spiritual growth is the real business of the church.

Every church needs ideological diversity. Churches today should be bringing about love and understanding between liberals and conservatives, the way that churches in former centuries needed to bring about love and understanding between Jews and Gentiles. This kind of spiritual unifying is a vital function of the church.

When spiritual vision becomes confused, churches tend toward one or another extreme: fundamentalism or secularization. The fundamentalists emphasize the *spiritual* but not *growth*: either you're saved or you're not. Apocalyptic rescue or punishment is coming soon for everyone. The secularizers see the need for *growth* but they include everything in it, diluting the *spiritual* into a generalized idealism for the betterment of the world. To this kind of religion, "spiritual growth" means anything, and the business of religion is everything.

Politics and religion will overlap in the life of every *individual*, but they should be kept separate on the level of the *group*, so that each group can more successfully pursue its own assignment. This is sometimes a difficult separation to make, but it must be made in order to avoid the tyrannies of theocracy on the one hand, and secularism on the other—wherein either confused religious values or degraded cultural values are imposed upon people, as in the ayatollahs' Iran or under communism, respectively. Whenever Caesar claims that which is God's he causes untold misery. And when religious groups overstep their bounds, they become political groups competing for Caesar-like power.

Yes, God is present in history; yes, social progress is part of the mandate to become more perfect; yes, the spiritual world endeavors to remake the material world into its likeness. No, this does not make social progress the direct business of religion; it only establishes a little-understood connection.

By centering the religious life in personality and its relation to God, Jesus laid the basis for all-around progress in all the things that personality does. His spirituality is "the light of the world" (Matt 5:14), giving insight to the mind, fire to the heart, warmth to the home, brother/sisterliness to society. "Your kingdom come. Your will be done, on earth as it is in heaven" (Matt 6:10) is a prophecy of the new world that will eventually be brought about when the "leaven" has worked its way through the bread: transforming the dough from within (Matt 13:33).

This is the challenge: can religion have a clear consciousness of spiritual purpose without falling into dogmatism, and have up-to-date relevancy without secularizing its message? Can it be the light of the world in a changing world? Can we identify with eternal truth, while admitting that our knowledge of truth must always grow? Can we work on eliminating interreligious hostilities?

Religion is not a social program, but a personal spiritual experience. Yet society cannot long remain livable without that heart of religious living throbbing inside it. Religion provides a beacon-light of spiritual idealism, spiritual stability amidst change.

WORLD PEACE

I have spoken of the ethics and fundamentals of spiritual unity. I would be remiss if I did not add some biblical wisdom about peace. Biblical peace entails peace with God ("we have peace with God through our Lord Jesus Christ," Rom 5:1; "Those of steadfast mind you keep in peace," Isa 26:3); peace with others ("be at peace with one another," Mark 9:50; "be at peace with all," Rom 12:18); and peace with ourselves ("my peace I give to you . . . let not your heart be troubled," John 14:27; "in me you may have peace," John 16:33).

There is a deep psychological link between having peace with God, peace with others, and peace with oneself. Violent dictators have a profound spiritual unrest and dis-ease that eats away at them, and they project this unease into outward aggression. This does not mean that world peace must await the day that all nations are ruled only by spiritually vibrant and insightful persons, but it probably *does* mean that the leading nations must be led by mentally balanced people who have *some* wisdom, self-restraint, and commitment to peace. There are many pragmatic and common-sense reasons for nations to instantiate peaceful procedures amongst themselves.

What, then, can we say about world peace?

The events of recent years have stimulated apocalyptic expectations in the population. But the greatest apocalyptic hope is for the final triumph of goodness, and that seems further off than ever. Many people hope for an end to this world, and the divine inauguration of a new one.

It is unlikely that peace will come from that avenue, nor from weak hopes for "international cooperation" such as the UN promotes. The plain fact is that social peace only comes through government, through the rule of law. World peace, therefore, cannot even be helpfully discussed apart from the idea of representative world government and enforceable world law.

Society's realization of the need for world government will not be a religious awakening so much as a practical recognition of what is necessary for survival. As we come closer to another world war, this awareness will grow.

Spiritually speaking, religion supports world unity; politically speaking, it must remain in the background. Religious values form the essential underpinning of worldwide brotherhood, but actual political unity is a political task. There are many people whose motive for peace is not consciously religious, nor need it be in order to help bring it about. The majority of the world's power brokers are not overly concerned with religious values anyway, and it is *they* who must make the move. Creating "good will among men" is a religious task, while creating "peace on earth" is a secular one, at least in terms of the institutional structures necessary for peace; the personal motivations for peace undoubtedly include religious ones.

Nevertheless, the process needs the assistance of religious fellow-feeling, because "men must be governed by God or they will be ruled by tyrants."[81] But as far as societies are concerned, the principle is: "If nations are not restrained by world law, they will be destroyed by war."

Thus the paradox of religion and world unity: empowered religion contributes to world unity, but it dare not take the front seat in driving us toward world government. It needn't anyway, because war and catastrophe are going to drive us quickly to the brink where we must choose between world government and world war. Religion's job is to teach us to love, and that job will be far from complete even after a successful world government puts an end to war.

Political groups and individuals need to take up the cry, using plain, worldly logic to get across the need for democratic world government that protects fundamental liberties, including religious liberty. The suppression of religious freedom smothers good will in a society and ensures the dominance of a warlike tendency. Witness Russia today, where many religious minorities are repressed.

Ever since Leo XIII's endorsement of the Conference of Nations in 1899, popes have been advocating for diplomatic solutions to prevent major wars. In 1952, Pius XII wrote "It is precisely the desire to forestall threatening conflicts which urges for the formation of a supernational juridical community."[82] Pope Francis

81. Frequently attributed to William Penn, but James Billington says "it has not been found in Penn's writings." Billington, *Respectfully Quoted*, 145.

82. From Wright, "Peace, International," 42.

continues this hope, writing in the encyclical *Fratelli Tutti* that the nations need "to submit their governmental powers to a reformed and more powerful United Nations in the hope of leading to one world government to benefit all mankind."[83]

Einstein made the same points, and it was in fact his passionate mission in the later years of his life. "A world government must be created which is able to solve conflicts between nations by judicial decision."[84] What is needed is "an international court of justice," but "the best court of justice is meaningless unless it is backed by the authority and power to execute its decisions, and exactly the same thing is true of a world parliament."[85] "The ultimate goal is the denationalization of military power altogether."[86]

Obviously, there is a boatload of obstacles and barriers standing in the way of even a minimal world government. Under pressure of an emergency, some of these barriers may subside. It may begin as an emergency measure to prevent imminent nuclear war. The formation of an actual World Court and World Parliament will take focused political will to do what is needed to have a process that will replace military confrontations. The age of military adventurism and bullying must be replaced by the rule of law. World peace requires world law. World law requires world government.

Also obvious is the fact that there are severe problems with national governments around the world today. What would make for a change in the way that national governments treat the populations? How can we prevent the kind of massacres being carried out in Myanmar, or the surveillance state, torture, and brainwashing in places like China and North Korea? There will be no overnight cure, but it is true that if national governments knew they were not going to be attacked by neighboring states, one of the reasons for their hyper-protectiveness would be removed. A world government could take an interest in protecting persecuted minorities, as US and Kurdish forces acted to protect the Yazidis in 2015–17

83. *Tomorrow's World.*

84. Einstein, *Out of My Later Years*, 138.

85. Einstein, *Out of My Later Years*, 141.

86. Einstein, *Out of My Later Years*, 143.

when they were being massacred by ISIS. A world government would need to combat terrorism and rogue states. A world government is not a panacea, but is simply the only way to prevent more world wars.

One peace group is Citizens for Global Solutions, descended from the World Federalist Institute. Some of their leaders include Madeleine Albright, Martin Sheen, Helen Caldicott, and theologian Gary Dorrien. They advocate changing the United Nations into a United Federation of Nations, adding an elected Parliament to represent the people of the world. The General Assembly could continue to represent the nations of the world. National governments would continue to exist, but would not have the right to wage war. There would be a strong international judicial system and states would "conform to universal human rights standards."[87]

This subject deserves its own book, a political science book. Here, in a theological book, it receives only limited space. National leaders who will some day agree to a governmental body with sovereign power to prevent war will be motivated primarily by worldly and practical motives, I think. Most of them will not be deep theological thinkers. The Bahá'í are more spiritually idealistic on this point than I am.

BAHÁ'Í

The religion that most directly and repeatedly emphasizes the ideal of the spiritual uniting of humanity is Bahá'í, which originated in the nineteenth century in Iran. The "oneness of humankind" is a central principle. Their founding prophet, Bahá'u'lláh, compared humanity to the human body, and said that the parts of the body do not compete but cooperate for survival and health. Abdu'l-Bahá, the head of the Bahá'í Faith from 1892 to 1921, emphasized the oneness of humanity: "In reality all are members of one human family—children of one Heavenly Father."[88] In 1938, Shoghi Effen-

---

87. Global Solutions.
88. 'Abdu'l-Bahá, *Abdu'l-Bahá On Divine Philosophy*, 26.

di, the Guardian of the Bahá'í Faith, said that "unity in diversity" was the "watchword" for the religion.[89]

The Bahá'í faith teaches "the oneness of God and religion . . . the progressive revelation of religious truth . . . the harmony between religion and science," and speaks of "ever-advancing civilization" and of "humanity advanc[ing] toward its collective maturity."[90]

Early leaders of the Bahá'í community wrote letters to world leaders seeking to promote peace and dialogue. Unfortunately, the community was persecuted in its native country, Iran, but it has spread throughout the world, and has about seven million followers. World peace is a primary goal of this religion: "Unbridled nationalism, as distinguished from a sane and legitimate patriotism, must give way to a wider loyalty, to the love of humanity as a whole."[91] All forms of prejudice are harmful to the eventual emergence of world peace.

Out of a desire for truth and a concern for the plight of humanity, religious leaders could put aside their religious differences and agree to work together for understanding and peace. "In essence, peace stems from an inner state supported by a spiritual or moral attitude."[92] "Universal acceptance of this spiritual principle [the oneness of mankind] is essential to any successful attempt to establish world peace."[93] This calls for a reconstruction and demilitarization of the whole world. Shoghi Effendi spoke of "the inevitable curtailment of unfettered national sovereignty as an indispensable preliminary to the formation of the future Commonwealth of all the nations of the world[.] Some form of a world superstate must needs be evolved, in whose favor all the nations of the world will have willingly ceded every claim to make war."[94] There needs to be a world parliament elected by the people of the

89. Effendi, *World Order of Bahá'u'lláh*, 41–42.

90. "Bahá'í Faith."

91. "Bahá'í Faith," section 2.

92. "Bahá'í Faith," section 2.

93. "Bahá'í Faith," section 3.

94. "Bahá'í Faith," section 3.

various countries. There must be a covenant, a "Union of the nations of the world."[95] The early stages of this arrangement will be "forced upon the world by the fear of nuclear holocaust." Beyond that will come the spiritual understanding that makes for a real "urge towards unity," and not just an emergency arrangement.[96] "We need to create a commonwealth of nations with an effective international tribunal for settling disputes peacefully."[97] The Baháʼís affirm unity not uniformity. World peace does not mean world homogenization.

"The teaching emphasizes the unity of humanity transcending all divisions of race, gender, caste, and social class, while celebrating its diversity. . . . One of the main principles of the Baháí Faith that comes about from the unity of humanity is the elimination of all forms of prejudice. . . . In this view, the fundamental purpose of society is spiritual and is to create a society that is favourable to the healthy development of all its peoples."[98]

The Baháʼís respect the founders of all the great religions, and believe that God spoke through them. "The religions of the world come from the same source and are in essence successive chapters of one religion from God."[99] Baháʼuʼlláh expressed great respect for Jesus. "He shed the splendor of His glory upon all created things. Through Him the leper recovered from the leprosy of perversity and ignorance. Through Him the unchaste and wayward were healed. Through His power, born of Almighty God, the eyes of the blind were opened and the soul of the sinner sanctified."[100] Each of the great religious founders was "a Manifestation of God" and "a skilled physician" for what ailed humanity. God is "the All-Knowing Physician."[101]

95. "Baháí Faith," section 3.
96. "Baháí Faith," section 4
97. "Bahai Teachings."
98. "Baháí Faith and the Unity of Humanity."
99. "Bahai Faith."
100. "Bahai.us."
101. "Bahai Faith."

Such a teaching will not suffice theologically for anyone who believes in the unique divinity of Jesus, but it is helpful that Jesus is treated as a truth revealer. It makes respectful conversation possible. Jesus himself said, "Whoever is not against us is for us" (Mark 9:40).

NEW GROUPS

The United Religions Initiative is a group founded in 2000, formed around small Cooperation Circles composed of "at least seven members from at least three religions, spiritual expressions, or indigenous traditions," who work on subjects like religious tolerance, peacebuilding, intercultural dialogue, community building, and care for the environment.[102] Groups may work on projects such as Jewish-Muslim dialogue, neighborhood peace, education, or human rights. The group partners with a number of UN organizations, the Parliament of the World's Religions, and the Institute for Economics and Peace.[103] Some high-profile figures (the late Hon. George Schultz, Gen. James Mattis, businessman Robert Lurie) have served on the Senior Advisory Council. The late Bishop William Swing was the President and a founding trustee. Thus, it is a group that has both grassroots membership and well-connected leadership.

I've already mentioned the Church of Conscious Harmony in Austin, Texas, which is open to the treasures of other religions while retaining a "deeply rooted faith in our own tradition."[104] Christians can draw upon the wisdom in other traditions, just as we have drawn on the faith of the Magi and on the honest questing of the Samaritan woman at the well.

Many groups can be part of a large cooperative endeavor that will yield peaceful results. Learning to recognize spiritual motivation in others is crucial to the unity we need.

---

102. United Religions Initiative.
103. United Religions Initiative.
104. Genung, "Finding Harmony," 25.

SPIRITUAL PROGRESS

I stated above that what will really be persuasive to the people of all religions is not Christian doctrine but the character of Jesus, the most compelling and interesting person in human history. His parables have been particularly persuasive, since they use down-to-earth characters to picture permanent spiritual truths. He is also appealing because he was always so interested in other people. He would stop what he was doing to minister to any person who approached him with spiritual need. If we uphold the image of Jesus the friend and kindly teacher, it will probably go further than any systematic doctrine about him. If we retell the stories of how he interacted with people, that will reach more people than any salvation formulas that we try to push. Some of the stories we tell will make it clear that Jesus is divine, and that is a by-product of telling the story. I don't think we need to impose any social obligations, any need to join or to pledge anything, any creed that needs to be repeated. Just tell the stories of Jesus, and he will appeal to human hearts.

Yoder insists that we must proclaim the real Jesus, "the Jewish Jesus of the New Testament . . . there is no alternative but painstakingly, feebly, repentantly, patiently, locally, to disentangle that Jesus from the Christ of Byzantium and of Torquemada."[105] The problem with past interfaith encounter was its imposition of empire and its distortion of Christ. The solution is not to be embarrassed to use the name of Jesus, but rather to reject the Constantinian Christ and return to the biblical Jesus. "The adjustment to Christendom's loss of élan and credibility is not to talk less about Jesus and more about religion but the contrary."[106]

Our greatest testimonies are two: the four gospels, and our own lives. For our lives are a living testimony of faith in Jesus. If we let the real Jesus be seen, he will eventually win over the human race. "When the Son of Man comes, will he find faith on earth?" (Luke 18:8). When there is more faith on earth, there will be more

---

105. Yoder, "Disavowal of Constantine," 261.
106. Yoder, "Disavowal of Constantine," 257.

readiness to recognize and receive Jesus. When he finds a predominance of faith on earth, it will be like a new world, where no one cries alone, where tears are wiped away. There is a resurrection coming for the human race, though probably not in my lifetime. But there will come that day when "love has been perfected among us" (1 John 4:17), and that will be like a remaking of the world. Perfect love will cast out fear. Jews and Gentiles, Russians and Chinese, black and white will acknowledge the sovereignty of God, and humbly set about to learn the practice of love. We need to recognize that God is a Nurturing Parent, and not a tyrannical one.

The human race needs to make spiritual progress. As Gregory of Nazianzus said:

> The Old Testament proclaimed the Father quite clearly, and the Son only dimly. The New Testament revealed the Son and allowed us to glimpse the divinity of the Spirit. Now the Spirit dwells among us and shows himself more clearly. . . . It was necessary therefore to work toward perfection by stages, by an "upward journey" to use David's phrase; it was necessary to go forward by way of successive clarification, by increasingly enlightening improvements and advances, in order to see the light of the Trinity shine out at last.[107]

Progress is the mandate of evolution. Spiritual progress is the mandate of spiritual evolution. The Master expects us to make a spiritual profit on the talents that he invested in us. Discipleship requires progress, which Jesus pictured as parallel to the growth of wheat: "The earth produces of itself, first the stalk, then the head, then the full grain in the head" (Mark 4:28).

Rahner sees a linkage between salvation and spiritual perfecting: "Man's final and definitive state, his salvation, the immortality of the soul or the resurrection of the flesh . . . when correctly understood, all of these terms are describing a final and definitive state of fulfillment for the cosmos."[108]

---

107. Gregory of Nazianzus, *Fifth Theological Discourse* 26; quoted in Dupuis, *Toward Religious Pluralism*, 42.

108. Rahner, *Foundations of Christian Faith*, 190.

The Spirit is active within the human race. I see the Spirit implied in the prophecy: "as a garden causes what is sown in it to spring up, so the Lord God will cause righteousness and praise to spring up before all the nations" (Isa 61:11). Progress will not seem so impossible if we believe that "The intrinsic purpose of evolution is growth toward goodness, beauty, and truth."[109] There is the assertion of Athanasius: "The Logos became a human being for the sake of our salvation [. . .] to set free all beings in himself, to lead the world to the Father and to pacify all beings in himself, in heaven and on earth."[110]

This is a biblical promise. "The earth will be filled with the knowledge of the glory of the Lord, as the waters cover the sea" (Hab 2:14). "He has made known to us the mystery of his will . . . set forth in Christ, as a plan for the fullness of time, to gather up all things in him, things in heaven and things on earth . . . until all of us come to the unity of the faith and of the knowledge of the Son of God, to maturity" (Eph 1:9–10; 4:13). "You . . . may become participants in the divine nature" (2 Pet 1:4). "Nation shall not lift up sword against nation, neither shall they learn war any more" (Isa 2:4).

109. McIntosh, *Evolution's Purpose*, 160.
110. *Letter to Adelphius*, PG 26.1081, quoted in Ramelli, *Larger Hope?*, 88.

Bibliography

1 Enoch: The Hermeneia Translation. George W. E. Nickelsburg and James C. VanderKam. Minneapolis: Fortress, 2012.

'Abdu'l-Bahá. *Abdu' l-Bahá On Divine Philosophy.* Compiled by Isabel Fraser Chamberlain. Boston: Tudor, 1918.

Arnold, Clinton E. *The Colossian Syncretism: The Interface between Christianity and Folk Belief at Colossae.* WUNT Second Series 77. Tübingen: Mohr Siebeck, 1995.

Athanasius. *Fourth Discourse Against the Arians.* From NPNF 2, vol. 4, 1892, 805–1101. Edited by Philip Schaff and Henry Wace. Reprint, Peabody, MA: Hendrickson, 1994.

Audo, Bishop Antoine. "Reflections (Middle East)." In *Let Mutual Love Continue (Hebrews 13:1): Report of the Third Global Gathering of the Global Christian Forum; Bogota, Columbia, 24–27 April 2018,* edited by Larry Miller, 173–77. Bonn: Global Christian Forum, 2021.

Augustine. *The City of God.* In *Basic Writings of Saint Augustine, Volume Two.* Edited by Whitney J. Oates. New York: Random House, 1948.

"The Bahá'í Faith." https://www.bahai.org/ and pages within that website.

"Baháí Faith and the Unity of Humanity." https://en.wikipedia.org/wiki/Bah%C3%A1%CA%BC%C3%AD_Faith_and_the_unity_of_humanity.

Bahai Teachings. https://bahaiteachings.org/ and pages within that website.

Bahai.us. https://www.bahai.us/ and pages within that website.

Bateman, Christian H., and Randall DeBruyn. "Come, Christians, Join to Sing."

Beeley, Christopher A. "Christ and Human Flourishing in Patristic Theology." *Pro Ecclesia* 25 (2016) 126–53.

Berdyaev, Nikolas. *The Beginning and the End.* London: Geoffrey Bles, 1947.

———. *Christian Existentialism.* Translated and selected by Donald A. Lowrie. New York: Harper and Row, 1965.

———. *The Destiny of Man.* Translated by Natalie Duddington, 1955. Reprint, New York: Harper and Row, 1960.

Bhagavati, Ma Jaya Sati. "How the AIDS Pandemic Changed My Life." In *Awakening the Spirit, Inspiring the Soul: 30 Stories of Interspiritual*

Discovery in the Community of Faiths, edited by Brother Wayne Teasdale and Martha Howard, 62–65. Woodstock, VT: Skylight Paths, 2004.

Billington, James. *Respectfully Quoted: A Dictionary of Quotations Requested from the Congressional Research Service*. Washington, DC: Library of Congress, 1989.

Blenkinsopp, Joseph. *Opening the Sealed Book: Interpretations of the Book of Isaiah in Late Antiquity*. Grand Rapids: Eerdmans, 2006.

Bowne, Borden Parker. *Personalism*. Boston: Houghton, Mifflin and Company, 1908.

Boyarin, Daniel. *A Radical Jew: Paul and the Politics of Identity*. Berkeley: University of California Press, 1994.

Bright, John. *The Kingdom of God: The Biblical Concept and Its Meaning for the Church*. Nashville: Abingdon, 1953.

Brightman, Edgar Sheffield. *The Spiritual Life*. New York: Abingdon-Cokesbury, 1942.

Brown, Peter. *The Body and Society: Men, Women and Sexual Renunciation in Early Christianity*. Lectures on the History of Religions 13. New York: Columbia University Press, 1988.

Case-Winters, Anna. *God Will Be All in All: Theology through the Lens of Incarnation*. Louisville: Westminster John Knox, 2021.

Citizens for Global Solutions. https://globalsolutions.org/federation/embracing-a-united-federation-of-nations/.

Clapp, Rodney. *Naming Neoliberalism: Exposing the Spirit of Our Age*. Minneapolis: Fortress, 2021.

Cobb, John B., Jr., and David Ray Griffin. *Process Theology: An Introductory Exposition*. Lousville: Westminster John Knox, 1976.

Cobb, John B., Jr., and C. Ives, eds. *The Emptying God: A Buddhist-Jewish-Christian Conversation*. Maryknoll, NY: Orbis, 1990.

Collins, John J. *Jewish Wisdom in the Hellenistic Age*. OTL. Louisville: Westminster John Knox, 1997.

D'Costa, Gavin. "The Impossibility of a Pluralist View of Religions." *Religious Studies* 32 (1996) 223–32.

Delio, Ilia. "Evolution and the Rise of the Secular God." In *From Teilhard to Omega: Co-creating an Unfinished Universe*, edited by Ilia Delio, 37–52. Maryknoll, NY: Orbis, 2014.

De Lubac, Henri, notes and commentary in Pierre Teilhard de Chardin and Maurice Blondel. *Pierre Teilhard de Chardin/Maurice Blondel Correspondence*. Translated by William Whitman. New York: Herder & Herder, 1967.

Dinges, William D., and Ilia Delio. "Teilhard de Chardin and the New Spirituality." In *From Teilhard to Omega: Co-creating an Unfinished Universe*, edited by Ilia Delio, 166–83. Maryknoll, NY: Orbis, 2014.

Donaldson, Terence L. *Judaism and the Gentiles: Jewish Patterns of Universalism (to 135 CE)*. Waco, TX: Baylor University Press, 2007.

Drum, David. *Peace Talks: The Good News of Jesus in a Donkey Elephant War*. Tucson: J17 Ministries, 2020.

Dunn, James D. G. *The Theology of Paul the Apostle*. Grand Rapids: Eerdmans, 1998.

Dupuis, Jacques. *Toward a Christian Theology of Religious Pluralism*. Maryknoll, NY: Orbis, 1997.

Edwards, Denis. *Breath of Life: A Theology of the Creator Spirit*. Maryknoll, NY: Orbis, 2004.

———. "Teilhard's Vision as Agenda for Rahner's Christology." In *From Teilhard to Omega: Co-creating an Unfinished Universe*, edited by Ilia Delio, 53–66. Maryknoll, NY: Orbis, 2014.

Effendi, Shoghi . *The World Order of Bahá'u'lláh*. Wilmette, IL: Bahai Publishing Trust, 1938.

Einstein, Albert. *Out of My Later Years*. New York: Citadel, 1956, 1984.

Epictetus. *The Discourses*. In *The Stoic and Epicurean Philosophers*, edited and translated by Whitney J. Oates, 221–386. New York: The Modern Library, 1940.

Fackre, Gabriel. "Divine Perseverance." In *What About Those Who Have Never Heard? Three Views on the Destiny of the Unevangelized*, edited by John Sanders, 71–95. Downers Grove, IL: IVP Academic, 1995.

Finlan, Stephen. *The Apostle Paul and the Pauline Tradition*. Collegeville, MN: Liturgical, 2008.

———. *Salvation Not Purchased: Overcoming the Ransom Idea to Rediscover the Original Gospel Teaching*. Eugene, OR: Cascade, 2020.

———. "Second Peter's Notion of Divine Participation." In *Theōsis: Deification in Christian Theology*, edited by Stephen Finlan and Vladimir Kharlamov, 32–50. PTM 52. Eugene, OR: Pickwick, 2006.

Forsyth, P. T. *The Person and Place of Jesus Christ*. Cincinnati: Jennings & Graham, 1909.

Frankl, Viktor. *Man's Search for Meaning*. New York: Washington Square, 1963.

Genung, Jeff. "Finding Harmony in the Spiritual Journey." In *Awakening the Spirit, Inspiring the Soul: 30 Stories of Interspiritual Discovery in the Community of Faiths*, edited by Brother Wayne Teasdale and Martha Howard, 22–27. Woodstock, VT: Skylight Paths, 2004.

Global Solutions. https://globalsolutions.org/federation/embracing-a-united-federation-of-nations/.

Gregory of Nyssa. OrthodoxWiki page. https://orthodoxwiki.org/Gregory_of_Nyssa.

Griffin, David. *Religion and Scientific Naturalism, Overcoming the Conflicts*. Albany, NY: SUNY Press, 2000.

Harink, Douglas. *Paul among the Postliberals: Pauline Theology Beyond Christendom and Modernity*. Grand Rapids: Brazos, 2003.

Hartshorne, Charles. *The Divine Relativity: A Social Conception of God*. New Haven: Yale University Press, 1948.

———. *Reality as Social Process*. Glencoe, IL: Free Press, 1953.

Hauerwas, Stanley, and William H. Willimon. *Resident Aliens: Life in the Christian Colony.* Nashville: Abingdon, 1989.

Haughey, John C. "Teilhard de Chardin: The Empirical Mystic." In *From Teilhard to Omega: Co-creating an Unfinished Universe,* edited by Ilia Delio, 203–17. Maryknoll, NY: Orbis, 2014.

Haught, John F. *Christianity and Science.* Maryknoll, NY: Orbis, 2007.

———. *The Cosmic Vision of Teilhard de Chardin.* Maryknoll, NY: Orbis, 2021.

———. *The John Haught Reader.* Eugene, OR: Wipf & Stock, 2018.

———. *Resting on the Future: Catholic Theology for an Unfinished Universe.* London: Bloomsbury, 2015.

———. *The New Cosmic Story: Inside Our Awakening Universe.* New Haven: Yale University Press, 2017.

Hays, Richard B. *Echoes of Scripture in the Letters of Paul.* New Haven: Yale University Press, 1989.

Heie, Harold. *Let's Talk: Bridging Divisive Lines through Inclusive and Respectful Conversations.* Eugene, OR: Cascade, 2021.

Heim, S. Mark. *Salvations: Truth and Difference in Religion.* Faith Meets Faith. Maryknoll, NY: Orbis, 1995.

Hick, John. *A Christian Theology of Religions: The Rainbow of Faiths.* Louisville: Westminster John Knox, 1995.

———. *Problems of Religious Pluralism.* London: Palgrave/Macmillan, 1985.

Höffding, Harald. *The Philosophy of Religion.* Translated by B. E. Meyer. London: Macmillan, 1906.

Irenaeus. *Against Heresies.* In ANF, volume 1, 1885, 309–567. Edited by Philip Schaff. Reprint, Grand Rapids: Eerdmans, 2001.

Jang, Se-Hoon. *Particularism and Universalism in the Book of Isaiah: Isaiah's Implications for a Pluralistic World from a Korean Perspective.* Bible in History. Bern: Peter Lang, 2005.

John Paul II, Pope. Statement at the World Day of Prayer for Peace. *Bulletin* (Secretariat for Non-Christians) 64/22/1 (1987) 54–62.

Kelly, J. N. D. *Early Christian Doctrines.* Rev. ed. New York: Harper & Row, 1978.

King, Ursula. *Towards a New Mysticism: Teilhard de Chardin and Eastern Religions.* New York: Seabury, 1980.

Knitter, Paul F. *Jesus and the Other Names: Christian Mission and Global Responsibility.* Maryknoll, NY: Orbis, 1996.

Köstenberger, Andreas J., and T. Desmond Alexander. *Salvation to the Ends of the Earth: A Biblical Theology of Mission.* 2nd ed. New Studies in Biblical Theology 53. Downers Grove, IL: IVP Academic, 2020.

Lao Tzu, *Tao te Ching.* Translated by James Legge. Sacred Books of the East 39. Oxford: Oxford University Press, 1891.

Lewis, C. S. *The Abolition of Man: How Education Develops Man's Sense of Morality,* 1947. Reprint, New York: Macmillan, 1955.

Ligneul, André. *Teilhard and Personalism.* Translated by Paul Joseph Oligny and Michael D. Meilach. Glen Rock, NJ: Paulist, 1968.

Lloyd-Jones, D. Martyn. *The Basis of Christian Unity*, 1962. Reprint, Edinburgh: Banner of Truth Trust, 2003.

MacDonald, Margaret Y. *The Pauline Churches: A Socio-historical Study of Institutionalization in the Pauline and Deutero-Pauline Writings.* Cambridge: Cambridge University Press, 1988.

MacLaren, Brian. *Why Did Jesus, Moses, the Buddha, and Mohammed Cross the Road?* New York: Jericho, 2012.

Mathewson, David. "Isaiah in Revelation." In *Isaiah in the New Testament,* edited by Steve Moyise and Maarten J. J. Menken, 189–210. London: T & T Clark, 2005.

Maudlin, Mickey. "Rob Bell's Hell." *NewsandPews,* July 2011. https://newsandpews.com/rob-bells-hell-by-mickey-maudlin-harperone-senior-v-p-executive-editor/.

McIntosh, Steve. *Evolution's Purpose: An Integral Interpretation of the Scientific Story of Our Origins.* New York: SelectBooks, 2012.

Michel, Thomas. T. "Bible Studies." In *Revisioning Christian Unity: Journeying with Jesus Christ, the Reconciler at the Global Christian Forum, Limuru, November 2007,* edited by Huibert van Beek, 102–8. Studies in Global Christianity. Eugene, OR: Wipf & Stock, 2009.

Moltmann, Jürgen. *The Spirit of Life: A Universal Affirmation.* Minneapolis: Fortress, 1992.

Nanak, Guru. *Japji Sahib* (Sikh Scripture). http://www.sikhs.nl/downloads/Nederlands/Jappu%20Ji%20Sahib_complete.pdf.

Neville, Robert C. "Nine Books by and about Teilhard." *Journal of the American Academy of Religion* 37 (1969) 71–82.

Panikkar, Raimon. *The Unknown Christ of Hinduism: Towards an Ecumenical Christophany.* London: Darton, Longman and Todd, 1981.

Philo of Alexandria. *On the Creation.* In *The Works of Philo, Complete and Unabridged,* 3–24. Translated by C. D. Yonge. New updated ed. Peabody, MA: Hendrickson, 1993.

———. *The Special Laws.* In *On the Decalogue: On the Special Laws; Books 1–3.* Translated by F. H. Colson. LCL 363. Cambridge: Harvard University Press, 1941.

Poole, Randall A. "Evgenii Trubetskoi and Russian Liberal Theology." In *Evgenii Trubetskoi: Icon and Philosophy,* edited by Teresa Obolevitch and Randall A. Poole, 25–51. Ex Oriente Lux 4. Eugene, OR: Pickwick, 2021.

Rahner, Karl. "Christianity and the Non-Christian Religions." In *A Rahner Reader,* edited by Gerald A. McCool, 214–20. New York: Seabury, 1975. Original source *Theological Investigations* V:118, 121–25, 127, 131–32.

———. *Foundations of Christian Faith: An Introduction to the Idea of Christianity.* Translated by William V. Dych. New York: Crossroad, 1978, 1997.

———. "Ideology and Christianity." In *A Rahner Reader,* edited by Gerald A McCool, 337–42. New York: Seabury, 1975. Original source *Theological Investigations* VI:43–45, 52–57.

————. "Jesus Christ. IV. History of Dogma and Theology." In *Encyclopedia of Theology: The Concise* Sacramentum Mundi, edited by Karl Rahner, 751–72. New York: Seabury, 1975.

————. "Jesus Christ," "Resurrection: D. Theology." In *Encyclopedia of Theology: The Concise* Sacramentum Mundi, edited by Karl Rahner, 1440–42. New York: Seabury, 1975.

Rambachan, Anantanand. "To Recognize and Love God in All: An Introduction to Hinduism." In *Five Voices, Five Faiths: An Interfaith Primer*, edited by Amanda Millay Hughes, 1–16. Cambridge: Cowley, 2005.

Ramelli, Ilaria L. E. *A Larger Hope? Universal Salvation from Christian Beginnings to Julian of Norwich.* Eugene, OR: Cascade, 2019.

Robinson, Bob. *Jesus and the Religions: Retrieving a Neglected Example for a Multi-Cultural World.* Eugene, OR: Cascade, 2012.

Rowland Jones, Sarah. "The Global Christian Forum—A Narrative History." In *Revisioning Christian Unity: Journeying with Jesus Christ, the Reconciler at the Global Christian Forum, Limuru, November 2007*, edited by Huibert van Beek, 3–37. Studies in Global Christianity. Eugene, OR: Wipf & Stock, 2009.

————. "The Global Christian Forum—A Narrative History: 'Limuru, Manado, and Onwards.'" *Transformation* 30 (2013) 226–42.

Sanders, John. *Embracing Prodigals: Overcoming Authoritative Religion by Embodying Jesus' Nurturing Grace.* Eugene, OR: Cascade, 2020.

————. "Inclusivism." In *What About Those Who Have Never Heard? Three Views on the Destiny of the Unevangelized*, edited by John Sanders, 21–55. Downers Grove, IL: IVP Academic, 1995.

Saucy, Mark. "Personal Ethics of the New Covenant: How Does the Spirit Change Us?" *Evangelical Quarterly* 86 (2014) 343–57.

Scott, Ernest F. *The Ethical Teaching of Jesus.* New York: Macmillan, 1924.

Simkovich, Malka L. *The Making of Jewish Universalism: From Exile to Alexandria.* Lanham, MD: Lexington, 2017.

Soloviev ("Solovyev"), Vladimir. *God, Man and the Church: The Spiritual Foundations of Life.* Translated by Donald Attwater. London: James Clarke & Co., 1938. (Originally 1882–84.)

————. ("Solovyov") *Lectures on Divine Humanity.* Revised and edited by Boris Jakim. Translated by Peter Zouboff. Hudson, NY: Lindisfarne, 1995.

Stark, Rodney. *The Triumph of Christianity: How the Jesus Movement Became the World's Largest Religion.* New York: HarperOne, 2011.

Starr, James M. *Sharers in Divine Nature: 2 Peter 1:4 in Its Hellenistic Context.* Coniectanea Biblical 33. Stockholm: Almqvist & Wiksell International, 2003.

Teilhard de Chardin, Pierre. "The Awaited Word." In *Toward the Future*, 92–100. Translated by René Hague. New York: Harcourt Brace Jovanovich, 1975.

————. *Christianity and Evolution.* Translated by René Hague. London: Collins, 1971.

———. "The Directions and Conditions of the Future." In *The Future of Man*, 227–37. Translated by Norman Denny. New York: Harper & Row: 1964.

———. *The Divine Milieu: An Essay on the Interior Life*. Translated by William Collins Sons & Co., Ltd. New York: Harper Torchbooks, 1960.

———. "Faith in Man." In *The Future of Man*, 185–92. Translated by Norman Denny. New York: Harper & Row: 1964.

———. "The Formation of the Noosphere: A Biological Interpretation of Human History." In *The Future of Man*, 155–84. Translated by Norman Denny. New York: Harper & Row: 1964.

———. *The Future of Man*. Translated by Norman Denny. New York: Harper & Row: 1964.

———. "The Grand Option." In *The Future of Man*, 37–60. Translated by Norman Denny. New York: Harper & Row: 1964.

———. *Human Energy*. Translated by J. M. Cohen. London: Collins, 1969.

———. *Let Me Explain*. Texts selected and arranged by Jean-Pierre Demoulin. Translated by René Hague and others. New York: Harper & Row, 1966.

———. "My Fundamental Vision." In *Toward the Future*, 163–208. Translated by René Hague. New York: Harcourt Brace Jovanovich, 1975.

———. "The Road of the West." In *Toward the Future*, 40–59. Translated by René Hague. New York: Harcourt Brace Jovanovich, 1975.

———. *Science and Christ*. Translated by René Hague. New York: Harper & Row, 1968.

———. "Some Reflections on Progress." In *The Future of Man*, 61–81. Translated by Norman Denny. New York: Harper & Row: 1964.

———. "The Spiritual Contribution of the Far East." In *Toward the Future*, 134–47. Translated by René Hague. New York: Harcourt Brace Jovanovich, 1975.

———. *Toward the Future*. Translated by René Hague. New York: Harcourt Brace Jovanovich, 1975.

Teilhard de Chardin, Pierre, and Maurice Blondel. *Pierre Teilhard de Chardin/ Maurice Blondel Correspondence*. Notes and commentary by Henri De Lubac. Translated by William Whitman. New York: Herder & Herder, 1967.

Tiemeyer, Lena-Sofia. "Death or Conversion: The Gentiles in the Concluding Chapters of the Book of Isaiah and the Book of the Twelve." *JTS* 68 (2017) 1–22.

Tomorrow's World. At https://www.tomorrowsworld.org/news-and-prophecy/pope-calls-for-one-world-government.

United Religions Initiative. https://www.uri.org/ and pages within that website.

Vacek, Edward. "An Evolving Christian Morality: *Eppur si muove*." In *From Teilhard to Omega: Co-creating an Unfinished Universe*, edited by Ilia Delio, 151–65. Maryknoll, NY: Orbis, 2014.

Ward, Keith. *Sharing in the Divine Nature: A Personalist Metaphysics*. Eugene, OR: Cascade, 2020.

Westermann, Claus. *Isaiah 40–66: A Commentary.* Translated by David M. G. Stalker. Philadelphia: Westminster, 1969.

Whitehead, Alfred North. *Adventures of Ideas.* New York: Macmillan, 1933.

———. "Immortality." In *The Philosoph y of Alfred North Whitehead*, edited by Paul A. Schilpp, 682–700. New York: Tudor, 1951.

———. *Process and Reality: An Essay in Cosmology*, 1929. Reprint, New York: Free Press, 1978.

Whitehead, Alfred North, and Lucien Price. *Dialogues of Alfred North Whitehead as Recorded by Lucien Price.* New York: Mentor, 1954.

Wilk, Florian. "Isaiah in 1 and 2 Corinthians." In *Isaiah in the New Testament*, edited by Steve Moyise and Maarten J. J. Menken, 133–58. London: T & T Clark, 2005.

Wright, J. J. "Peace, International: Modern Papal Teaching." In *New Catholic Encyclopedia, vol. XI*, edited by staff at Catholic University of America, 41–45. New York: McGraw Hill, 1967.

Yoder, John H. "The Disavowal of Constantine." In *The Royal Priesthood: Essays Ecclesiological and Ecumenical*, edited by Michael G. Cartwright, 243–61. Scottdale, PA: Herald, 1998.

———. "The Otherness of the Church." In *The Royal Priesthood: Essays Ecclesiological and Ecumenical*, edited by Michael G. Cartwright, 54–64. Scottdale, PA: Herald, 1998.

———. "Peace without Eschatology?" In *The Royal Priesthood: Essays Ecclesiological and Ecumenical*, edited by Michael G. Cartwright, 144–67. Scottdale, PA: Herald, 1998.

Subject Index

Names Index

Evagrius, 63

Fackre, Gabriel, 103
Finlan, Stephen, 25, 52, 79
Forsyth, P. T., 75
Francis, Pope, 116–17
Francis of Assisi, 84
Frankl, Viktor, 110

Gandhi, Mahatma, 101
Genung, Jeff, 107, 121
Gregory of Nazianzen, 62, 123
Gregory of Nyssa, 61–62
Griffin, David Ray, 83–87, 111

Harink, Douglas, 42, 105
Hartshorne, Charles, 84
Hauerwas, Stanley, 71
Haughey, John C., 78
Haught, John F. , 72, 74, 87–92
Hays, Richard B., 45
Heie, Harold, 68–69
Heim, S. Mark, 98–99, 103–5
Hick, John, 93–94, 96, 103–4
Höffding, Harald, 86

Irenaeus, x, 60, 63, 82
Ives, C., 97

Jang, Se-Hoon, 3–4, 11
John Paul II, Pope, 95, 100–1
Julian of Norwich, 62
Justin Martyr, 58–59, 94

Kelly, J. N. D., 58–59
King, Ursula, 75–77
Knitter, Paul F., 99–105
Köstenberger, Andreas J., 37

Lao Tzu, 111
Legge, James, 111
Leo XIII, Pope, 116
Lewis, C. S., 109–10
Ligneul, André, 30–31, 76, 80
Lloyd-Jones, D. Martyn, 49
Lurie, Robert, 121

MacDonald, Margaret Y., 52
Marcellus, 61
Mathewson, David, 53–54
Mattis, Gen. James, 121
Maudlin, Mickey, 93
McIntosh, Steve, 81, 86–87, 89–92, 124
Methodius, 60
Michel, Thomas, 70
Moltmann, Jürgen, 81
Mounier, Emmanuel, 30–31, 76

Nanak, Guru, 109
Neville, Robert C., 77–78

Oates, Whitney J., 64–65
Origen, 60–61
OrthodoxWiki Gregory of Nyssa page, 62

Penn, William, 116
Panikkar, Raimon, 97
Philo of Alexandria, 20, 23–24, 26
Pius XII, Pope, 116
Poole, Randall A., 65
Price, Lucien, 83
Pseudo-Phocylides, 20, 24–25

Rahner, Karl, 40, 78–79, 81, 94, 96, 123
Rambachan, Anantanand, 102
Ramelli, Ilaria L. E., 8, 52, 59–64, 124
Robinson, Bob, 14, 105–6
Rowland Jones, Sarah, 70
Rumi, Jalaluddin, 101

Sanders, John, 29, 67–68, 97
Saucy, Mark, 28
Scheler, Max, 76
Schultz, Hon. George, 121
Scott, Ernest F., 31
Seneca, 25
Sheen, Martin, 118
Simkovich, Malka, 19–25
Soloviev, Vladimir, 65–66, 88

Ancient Document Index

26:61	108	11:30	28
27:54	34	11:31	40
28:19	ix, 34–35, 61	12:32	68
		13:29	36

Mark

	13:30	36
2:22	29–30
3:35	29, 48, 57, 109
4:28	41, 123
5:1	27, 33
7:24–31	27
7:24–30	33
7:24	27
7:31	27, 33
9:40	107, 121
9:50	115
11:1–7	17, 32
11:15	32
11:17	9, 32, 55
12:35	x, 32
12:37	x, 32
13:10	33
14:9	33

13:34 36
14:23 36
17:18 x
18:8 122
22:30 68
23:34 67
24:47 ix, 36

John

1:3 38, 58
1:10 38
1:12 38
1:14 38
3:36 38
4:7–29 ix
5:25 103
6:35 38
6:45 61
7:17 29, 48, 109
10:9 103
10:16 31, 55
10:18 58
11:50 38
11:51–52 38
11:52 31
12:14–16 17
12:20–22 29
12:31 51
13:34–35 40
14:2–3 40
14:17 38
14:27 115
15:10 39
15:15 28, 39
15:26 38
16:13 38
16:33 39–40, 115
17 69
17:2 39
17:11 39

Luke

2:30–32 35
3:6 36, 48
4 106
4:18–19 35
4:18 106
4:21 106
4:25–27 35, 106
6:17 36
6:19 58
7:1–10 36
7:9 x, 36
8:15 29, 109
8:26 27, 33
8:37 33
9:49–50 108
9:54–55 x
10:18 51
10:25–37 x
10:29–37 ix
10:37 40

CPSIA information can be obtained
at www.ICGtesting.com
Printed in the USA
LVHW102220140323
741644LV00006B/449